LIFE INSURANCE

CONFIDENTIAL™

"Don't let yourself own a bad policy..."

AF719607

JOHN NGUYEN, EA, CLU® CHFC®

Licensed Life Insurance Analyst

Copyright © 2025 by LifeInsuranceReview.com

All rights reserved.

No part of this book may be reproduced, stored in a retrieval system, or transmitted in any form or by any means, electronic, mechanical, photocopying, recording, or otherwise, without the prior written permission of the author, except in the case of brief quotations used in reviews, articles, or educational settings with proper attribution.

This publication is for general informational purposes only. It does not constitute legal, tax, investment, or insurance advice. Readers should consult licensed professionals regarding their own personal, financial, or insurance planning before taking any action based on the content of this book.

The author has made every effort to ensure the accuracy of the information contained herein at the time of publication. However, laws, regulations, and financial products may change, and the author assumes no responsibility for any errors or for the outcomes of actions taken based on this information.

Self-published by LifeInsuranceReview.com
ISBN: 979-8-218-75183-8
Cover Design by: The LIR TEAM
Printed in USA

Life Insurance Confidential™ book series
is a trademark of John Nguyen & LifeInsuranceReview.com

For inquiries, speaking engagements, or bulk orders, please contact:
book@lifeinsurancereview.com

TABLE OF CONTENTS

Dedication 1

Foreword 3

The Great Introduction 5

Chapter One: Why Fiduciaries Matter: Guardians of Your Financial Future 35

Chapter Two: The Different Types of Life Insurance Explained 52

Chapter Three: Life Insurance is Fantastic (But Only if it Meets YOUR Goals!) 64

Chapter Four: Buy, Don't Be Sold: How the Industry Pushes Policies You Don't Need or are NOT the Best Value 79

Chapter Five: Policy Illustrations – The Danger of Assumptions and False Projections 98

Chapter Six: Conflicts of Interest and Ignorance – What They Don't Want You to Know 110

Chapter Seven: The Free Look Period – Your Last Line of Defense 127

Chapter Eight: Common Pitfalls and Hidden Costs in Life Insurance Policies 142

Chapter Nine: Life Changes, So Should Your Life Insurance 156

Chapter Ten: The Alternative – Why Term Life Insurance Is Often the Appropriate Choice 169

Chapter Eleven: How to Spot Red Flags and Protect Yourself 183

Chapter Twelve: How LifeInsuranceReview.com (LIR) Can Help Protect Your Family's Future 198

Conclusion: Empowerment Through Knowledge 222

Appendix: 12 Case Studies 229

Bonus and Notes 269

DEDICATION

To my valued clients—both personal and those of our firm. To my partners, team members, professional referral partners, mentors, and my super supportive and patient family, thank you.

Without each and every one of you, this three-year book journey would not have been possible. From the very beginning, when I got licensed in 2005, to the founding of LIR (Life Insurance Review) Insurance Solutions agency in 2011, your trust, guidance, and encouragement have shaped the course of my professional life.

I've learned so much from the collective wisdom of those who have generously shared their insights along the way. I'm especially grateful to those who believe in and support our vision and values: to always act as true advocates for the consumer.

Thank you for standing with us as we expanded our mission beyond traditional life insurance planning to focus on what truly matters: advocacy, education, and transparency.

Through all the dedicated work we've done together, we've built LIR to be more than just a service, it's a trusted resource. A place where consumers are empowered with clarity, not pressured by the life insurance sales industry, but equipped to make confident, informed purchasing decisions for themselves and their families.

I remain committed to growing both personally and professionally so that I may continue to live up to your expectations, and to be the best and truest advocate for consumers.

With deep gratitude,

FOREWORD

Welcome to ***Life Insurance Confidential*** — your guide to understanding and navigating the opaque world of life insurance sales.

You might wonder why we explore the "underbelly" of this industry, but the reasons are compelling. Too many people end up with policies that don't truly meet their needs or represent the best options available. This isn't always the result of bad actors or intentional deception. More often, the core issue lies not in how these life insurance products are designed, but in how they are promoted and sold, creating a false sense of having the best coverage and value, when in reality, they often fall short.

This book isn't about criticizing life insurance itself: it's about giving you insight into the sales industry behind it. Life insurance is a powerful financial product and tool when used correctly.

That's why I wrote this book: to give you the knowledge, resources, and insights to take control of the decision-making process. You should never feel like you're being steered into a policy because it benefits someone else's bottom line. Instead, you deserve the ability to explore your options, ask informed questions, and verify what you're being told and sold, whether it's coming from an agent, broker, or financial advisor.

In the life insurance sales world, hitting production targets often takes precedence over doing what is truly in the client's best interest. The consumer experience is built around sales strategies shaped by internal incentives such as bonuses, contests, and compensation structures that prioritize production over service. As a result, consumers have little to no real opportunity to be properly served and are often simply sold to.

So, is this book for you?

- If you're shopping for a policy—or have already shopped for one—and still haven't made a decision, this book is for you.
- If you're unsure which type of life insurance is truly right for your situation, this book is for you.
- If you or your loved one already own a policy but want to better understand it, this book is for you.
- If your policy is over two years old and hasn't been reviewed, this book is for you.
- If you're interested in learning more about how life insurance is sold, whether to protect yourself as a consumer or to explore it as a potential career done the right way, this book is for you.
- And if you purchased your policy from someone who is not a fiduciary or a licensed life insurance analyst, this book is especially for you—so you can understand the difference and make informed choices.

Let's begin. Together, we'll demystify the life insurance sales industry once and for all, so you can make informed, confident decisions and not be sold something you don't fully understand or truly need.

THE GREAT INTRODUCTION

The life insurance industry thrives on what-ifs;
your job is to separate the probable from the predatory.
— **Unknown**

If you're reading this book, chances are you've encountered one of these situations: you feel overwhelmed and confused by all the sales information about life insurance and what's best; you know you need life insurance but aren't sure which options are right for you; you already have a policy but question whether it truly meets your needs; or you were recently sold a policy and aren't certain it lives up to what was promised. In short, you've likely found yourself at the mercy of the life insurance sales industry, and that's a common experience.

The good news is, you don't have to be. This book will provide you with the knowledge to empower you to make clear decisions. After all, knowledge, when applied with purpose, is real power. My goal is to pull back the curtain on the life insurance sales industry. I think you will find this book not only insightful, but necessary. Life insurance is one of the most important financial products you'll ever purchase, yet the process of buying it often feels more like solving a riddle than making an informed decision. Why is that? Unfortunately, the life insurance industry does not require its agents and brokers to act as fiduciaries to consumers. Their primary role is sales, not unbiased guidance. I've been licensed in the industry for more than two decades, I'm here to cut through the perplexity to arm you with some untold knowledge and insight.

This book is designed to give you the confidence to take control of your life insurance decisions, empowering you to evaluate your options and choose the policy that best fits your needs, without relying on any sales pitch.

Life Insurance: A Critical, Yet Often Misunderstood "Asset"

Let's start with a hard truth: Life insurance is essential if you have loved ones who depend on you financially. It protects them from the burden of your financial responsibilities in the event of your premature passing. It doesn't have to be a glamorous purchase, but it can be a foundational one. Think about what life insurance does, it can guarantee that, should the worst happen, your family, your business, or your legacy can be protected. It can pay off debts, replace lost income, ensure your children can financially go to college, and/or even to protect your estate. That's a real peace of mind that you can purchase.

However, here's where it gets tricky: life insurance is often sold, not bought. Think about what this means. Many of us usually don't approach life insurance to buy like how we would with a brand new car or newly built house, with clear comparison points and plenty of information. The idea and need for life insurance is often pitched to us, as most of us don't even know it's an important personal asset to have, and we usually don't understand all of our options. When you don't know what you don't know, it's hard to make an informed decision!

For example, if you are to buy a brand new specific car, you usually will know what you need and what it looks like. A car for five people, decent storage capacity, safe, and reasonably priced. If you show up at the dealership and the salesperson tries to convince you that a two-seater Porsche is exactly the right car for you, you would be insulted. The Porsche, while arguably a dream car for some, does not meet your current goals, needs, or budget.

Hence, it's so important to know what you want and need. The knowledge of your needs and of the types of cars that are available on the market empowers you to know whether the salesperson's offer is right for you or not. That is the difference between buying what is right for you and being sold what the salesperson wants you to buy.

Let's move this analogy to being sold life insurance. Too often, you're sold on what an agent or broker thinks you should want, or worse, what they want you to buy because it may be more profitable for them in terms of their compensation structure.

The result? Unrealistic expectations. Confusion. Miscommunication. And in many cases, policies that don't meet or fall short of your needs. This book will give you the insights and tools to flip the script, empower you with more knowledge to buy life insurance on your terms, rather than being sold something or being told what is best for you instead.

Why This Book?

Whether you have received advice on life insurance from friends or the internet, remember, it never hurts to do more research! Your luck is in which source you encounter. Hopefully with this book, it can be a useful source to get you started and end on the right track for you!

The life insurance industry is complex, and it's easy for misinformation to spread. That's one reason why this book is necessary: it provides clarity. But more importantly, it helps you distinguish between the life insurance you truly need and the policies that are simply not a best fit—whether that's from a sales-driven agent or broker, a website advertisement inviting you to share your contact information to learn more, or a viral video pushing oversimplified solutions.

The Benefits of Life Insurance: Why It's a Personal Asset Like No Other

Before you get any silly ideas, our team and I love what life insurance can do and believe that most people need it. Life insurance isn't just about covering funeral expenses or replacing a year's salary. It's a multi-functional personal asset that can do things no other financial product or tool can. Let's look at a few examples:

- **Protecting Loved Ones:** The most obvious benefit is ensuring your family's financial stability. Life insurance can pay off your mortgage, eliminate debt, or provide an income stream to maintain your family's standard of living.
- **Living Benefits:** Some policies offer features like accelerated death benefits which you can access while you're still alive to cover for disability, long-term care, chronic, critical, and terminal illnesses.

- **Wealth Building:** Certain types of life insurance, like whole life or universal life policies, allow you to build cash value over time. This cash value grows tax-deferred and can be accessed through loans or withdrawals for various purposes tax-free, such as supplementing retirement income, funding a large purchase, seeding a business venture, or seizing investment opportunities. Unlike other personal or financial assets, the growth within a cash value policy isn't subject to annual taxation, making it an attractive option for long-term wealth accumulation.
- **Business Continuity:** If you're a business owner, life insurance can fund buy-sell agreements, pay off business debts, or provide cash to hire a replacement if a key employee or partner passes away.
- **Estate Planning:** For anyone who wants to transfer an additional tax-free asset to the next generation—or for those who already have significant assets—life insurance can help cover estate taxes, ensuring that your heirs receive the full benefit of your hard work.

When chosen carefully and designed properly, life insurance becomes more than a safety net, it's a tool for protecting and wealth building. But here's the catch: not all policies are created equal, and not all salespeople have your best interests at heart.

What You Need vs. What You're Sold

Here is the point where many people run into trouble. The life insurance policy you need is based on factors like your income, debts, dependents, and long-term goals. But the policy you're sold is often shaped by what's most profitable for the person and/or the company selling it. Let's unpack that.

Term Insurance vs. Permanent Insurance

You've probably heard of **term insurance**: it's simple, straightforward, and affordable. You pay for coverage over a specific period (say, 20 or 30 years), and if you pass away during that time, your beneficiaries receive the death benefit. This is often the best choice for young families or anyone with a limited budget.

Then there's permanent life insurance which includes whole life and universal life that provides lifelong coverage and builds cash value. It's sometimes marketed as an "additional savings asset" or an "alternative asset" with tax advantages. And while it has its place, it's often oversold to consumers who don't need it or can't afford the added charges and expenses, which in turn generates higher commissions for agents and brokers.

The reality? There's no one-size-fits-all solution. You may need term insurance, permanent life insurance, or a combination of both. But without a clear understanding of the pros and cons, you're at the mercy of the person selling you the policy.

Why Misinformation Persists

One reason life insurance remains so misunderstood is the industry's heavy reliance on jargon. Terms like 'building cash value,' 'living benefits,' 'flexible premiums,' 'tax-free,' and many other **phrases** are often used in vague ways. When you combine that with the sales-driven nature of the business, it creates an environment where consumers can easily be misled or taken advantage of.

To make matters worse, some agents rely on fear-based tactics. Questions like "What happens to your family if you die tomorrow?" are meant to put you on edge and cloud your judgment. When combined with pressure-based sales techniques, it's no surprise that so many people end up with policies they don't fully understand—often overpaying for coverage and features they may not even need.

Let's Demystify the Process

The goal of this book isn't to turn you into a life insurance product or planning expert. Trust me, becoming one took years of experience, multiple certifications, passing many exams, and staying current with extensive continuing education each year. But even all of that was only half of what's truly required. The other half came from specializing in life insurance product and policy reviews, handling complex planning cases, and working closely with clients over the past 20 years. That real-world experience has taught me how to empower others to become more informed and confident buyers of life insurance. By the time you finish this book, you'll know how to:

- Ask the right questions **to ensure** clear answers.
- Identify what type of life insurance you actually need.
- Compare policies effectively, cutting through the jargon.
- Spot red flags when being sold and in policy illustrations.
- Understand how life insurance fits into your overall financial plan.

More importantly, you'll walk away with confidence, the kind that comes from knowing you're making decisions based on clear information and just feelings. Our firm's motto is "explore, compare, and verify" and we want to give you the tools to do just that. I want you to go from believing that your life insurance policy is the best for you to knowing that it is.

Before we dive into the details, let's address one last thing: life insurance is too important to leave in the hands of influencers and algorithms. YouTube or TikTok might be a fun way to discover recipes or learn life hacks, but it should not be the place to find personalized life insurance advice. This book exists to provide a solid foundation, grounded in expertise and free of clickbait.

Redefining the Value of Life Insurance

Life insurance is one of the most significant financial decisions you'll make, yet it's a product too often misunderstood or misrepresented. According to author and podcaster Michael Hyatt, "Americans spend more time planning for their annual vacation than they do planning their financial future." Let that sink in.

One problem is that people don't see the value in a product that they may not be around to use. (I 100% do not think that this needs to be the case, but we will address that later in the book!) Instead, let's understand the value proposition of life insurance.

Value is inherently subjective. The true meaning of value is when the perception of worth exceeds the cost. What this means is that a life insurance policy that is of great value to me, may not be to you. My needs are completely different from yours. While my concern might be an affordable policy to protect my kids if I die unexpectedly, your concern could be ensuring your business can continue.

Though our needs are different, a great value to each of us is a life insurance policy that meets our specific needs at a price we are willing to pay.

This book will empower you to define what value in life insurance truly means for your unique situation, cutting through the noise of sales and confusing industry jargon to focus on what matters most: your needs and goals.

Understanding the challenges of the life insurance industry and the pitfalls of a sales-driven approach is the first step toward making informed, empowered decisions. Through my years in the business, I have seen the disasters that occur when people are sold to. We built our business to counter the mistakes we see in the life insurance sales industry so that you can find the value that works for you.

Specifically, our firm focuses on the key differences between advice versus counsel, emotion versus empowerment, and selling versus review.

The Misaligned Value of Life Insurance

For many consumers, the process of purchasing life insurance feels overwhelming. This is usually by design. Agents and brokers present complex products, emphasizing features, and riders that sound appealing. Life insurance is unlike other financial products; it's rarely researched and rarely chosen proactively by consumers. Instead, it's sold with recommendations that are often influenced by commissions, sales targets, additional production incentives, and the limited portfolio of products the salesperson can or wants to offer.

This sales-driven model creates significant risks to the consumer, including:

Commission-Driven Recommendations: Agents and brokers might steer you toward policies that offer higher commissions rather than those that are better suited to your needs, with greater coverage value and benefits compared to other options

Limited Choices: Agents tied to a single company's offerings or brokers who only represent a group of companies will not present the full range of available policies that may be best for your needs.

Potential Mismatches: Consumers often overpay for features they don't need or end up with insufficient coverage, leaving their loved ones with an insufficient death benefit.

Let's return to the Porsche example. A Porsche sports car certainly embodies exceptional racing performance and carries a price tag to match. While that price may be justified by what you get, if you need an affordable car to transport your family of five around the suburbs, a Porsche likely doesn't offer real value for your needs.

Similarly, life insurance policies are often sold based on company branding, long histories, financial ratings, and unique products that may not align with the practical needs of most consumers. For example, the cash value of permanent life insurance policies often falls short of the projections illustrated at the time of sale.

Adding Clarity to Empower Your Decisions

While the life insurance industry can often feel opaque, understanding how it operates empowers you to prioritize your needs over the sales incentives offered to your agent or broker. Here are some important facts to know: Many agents and brokers enter the industry with minimal training, spending their first few years focusing mostly on sales and marketing themselves, with little emphasis on product knowledge. Early on, most new agents and brokers are encouraged to sell primarily to their personal contacts, who are often the best prospects due to their trust and familiarity, despite sometimes overlooking the agent's limited knowledge and experience. High turnover rates, with over 80% of new agents leaving the field within their first few years, only worsen this problem, leaving clients without the long-term support needed to maintain and optimize their policies.

The Importance of Policy Reviews

Rather than relying solely on the advice of a single agent or broker, seeking an independent review of your life insurance policy can provide invaluable clarity. An unbiased second opinion helps you compare and understand a wider range of policy options, empowering you to make informed choices aligned with your financial goals. Remember: explore, compare, and verify!

Red Flags vs. Green Flags

From my 20+ years of experience, I have learned the life insurance sales industry is full of red flags. I decided to counteract those red flags with green flags of my own. The following "red flag vs green flag" comparisons are critical to ensuring that the life insurance policy you choose adds clear value to your financial plan:

1. Advice vs. Counsel

Advice: Often shaped by the salesperson's incentives, advice may lean toward specific products, regardless of their fit for your needs. It may sound like, "If I were you..." or "This is our best product..."

Counsel: An objective, fiduciary approach that puts your financial interests above all else. It's about empowering you to think independently rather than simply being told what's best for you. For example, a fiduciary professional ensures you clearly understand your needs and wants before presenting any options, making sure you have a solid grasp of the choices available. Above all, it's about always putting the client first.

2. Emotion vs. Empowerment

Emotion: Many sales tactics prey on fear and urgency, encouraging you to let emotions drive your decision-making. This often leads to purchasing a policy without fully understanding its terms or details, as the focus is on selling a single "best" solution that supposedly has no equal. Common pitches include questions like, "Don't you want your family taken care of if you die unexpectedly?" or claims that a specific product will solve all your concerns.

Empowerment: By first understanding your needs, wants, and long-term goals, you're in a better position to explore all available options and see how different types of life insurance can align with your overall financial plan. As part of this process, you'll evaluate cost-effective term policies with living benefits. When combined with investing the premium savings into a Roth IRA or Roth 401(k), this approach can provide greater long-term value, flexibility, and control. From there, you can also make meaningful comparisons to permanent policies with cash value to determine what's truly in your best interest.

3. Selling vs. Review

Selling: An approach focused on promoting a specific product and a fixed narrative about why it is the best, leaving little room for comparison. The goal is to get the prospect to trust only what is being presented, rather than encouraging independent thinking or exploration of other options.

Review: An independent review takes a comprehensive look at your financial situation, goals, and existing coverage to determine the most suitable life insurance solution for your needs. It goes beyond surface-level comparisons by identifying gaps, inefficiencies, or missed opportunities. For instance, a thorough review may uncover that your current policy lacks valuable features such as living benefits, or that it doesn't provide sufficient death benefit protection to meet your family's long-term needs.

Realigning Life Insurance with Your Needs

When you shift the focus from being sold a policy to actively choosing one that fits your needs, the value of life insurance becomes clearer. Here are some practical steps to take control of the process (and don't worry, we will cover all of this in detail later):

- **Seek Unbiased Advice:** Work with a fiduciary advisor or a company like LifeInsuranceReview.com (LIR). Since 2011, our firm has positioned itself as an independent consumer advocate, always putting the client's best interest first

- **Ask the Right Questions:** Make sure you fully understand what you're being told and sold. Use the question guide provided in this book, and ensure your questions are clearly answered so you have full clarity before taking any further steps.
- **Reevaluate Regularly:** Your needs and financial goals can change over time. Periodic reviews help ensure your policy continues to align with your current objectives. If you have a cash value policy, be sure to check that it's performing as expected and compare it to the original illustration provided at the time of sale.

Avoiding the Common Pitfalls

The consequences of being sold the wrong life insurance policy can be significant. The last thing you want to do is invest in a policy that does not give you the protections and benefits that you need.

Overpaying for Features

Complex policies, such as those with cash value components or included "accelerated death benefit riders," may sound appealing but can increase overall costs and often negatively impact cash value performance. For many consumers, simpler policies prove to be more cost-effective.

Insufficient Coverage

When agents and brokers prioritize commissions over delivering the best value to clients, consumers may miss out on policies that offer better coverage at similar prices. Imagine a policy that provides 40% more death benefit for the same cost; such opportunities are often overlooked due to the commission-driven and highly competitive nature of life insurance sales.

Confusion and Frustration

A lack of understanding about what was explained, sold, and the actual final policy at delivery leaves many consumers in the dark about what they've purchased, making it difficult to fully leverage the value of their life insurance.

The Path to True Value

Life insurance is more than just a product; it's a commitment to your family's financial security. By focusing on what you genuinely need, without succumbing to sales pressures, you can ensure your policy delivers long-term value. The difference lies in taking control of the process: educating yourself, seeking unbiased counsel, and prioritizing your financial goals above all else.

At LIR, we will empower you with the tools and knowledge to make smarter decisions, ensuring your policy aligns with your needs rather than the incentives of an agent or broker. With the right approach, you'll gain peace of mind knowing your family's future is secure.

Exposing the Obscured Realities of the Life Insurance Industry

Choosing a life insurance policy is one of the most critical financial decisions you'll make. Yet, the process is riddled with obscured motivations and conflicts of interest that benefit agents, brokers, and insurance companies far more than you. This book promises to lift the curtain on the life insurance sales industry, exposing it's bad practices and empowering you to make informed decisions based solely on what's best for you, not anyone else.

The Commission Game: When "Free" Isn't Free

A common selling point in the life insurance industry is that agents and brokers don't charge clients directly for their services. Instead, they earn commissions on the policies they sell, often paid as a percentage of your premium. While this arrangement seems convenient, it can introduce a potential conflict of interest.

Agents and brokers spend the **majority** of their time learning and perfecting their sales skills. They're incentivized to sell policies that offer the highest compensation, and that's simply human nature. I'm not even arguing they're trying to consciously deceive you. But people naturally gravitate toward where they'll be rewarded the most. The fact is, that might not be what's best for you.

This is especially true for complex, high-premium policies with features that sound beneficial but might not serve your actual needs. For example, a whole life policy with a cash value component may be aggressively marketed over a simpler term policy because it offers the agent a more lucrative commission structure.

This raises a fundamental question: Are agents and brokers genuinely prioritizing your best interests, or are they influenced by the policies that maximize their income? This book will give you the answer to that question. Even better, I have designed this book to help you navigate these obscured dynamics to find policies that serve your goals, not someone else's wallet.

Limited Options and Expertise

Another overlooked reality of the life insurance sales industry is the limitation of options often presented to consumers, although many consumers remain unaware of this. Many insurance sales professionals are "captive," meaning they represent a single insurance company and are restricted to selling only that company's products along with a limited number of approved others. While brokers generally have access to a wider range of products than captive agents, their recommendations may still be constrained by marketing affiliations, agency relationships, or insurer contracts. These restrictions can limit the full range of policy options they present to you.

This lack of comprehensive choice often results in policies that are suboptimal for consumers. For instance, a broker might suggest a policy with fewer benefits or higher premiums simply because it falls within their limited portfolio. Moreover, agents and brokers—particularly newer ones—may lack the financial planning expertise needed to recommend policies that align with your long-term goals, leaving you with coverage that fails to adapt to life's inevitable changes.

The bottom line is that you have to be equipped to assess whether an agent or broker is truly acting in your best interest.

The World of Network Marketing in Insurance

Beware of an increasingly prominent yet little-discussed aspect of the life insurance industry which is the rise of network marketing companies (also known as multi-level marketing or MLMs). These organizations often position themselves as independent agents or brokers, but their structure reveals a different motivation.

Representatives in these types of marketing organizations frequently act as marketers rather than true financial advisors. Their focus is twofold, one on recruiting people to join them so they sell to those new recruit's friends and family members. Two, focusing on hitting sales targets to achieve higher commission payout levels and earning perks like luxury gifts, vacations that are called leadership conferences, and many other incentives. While these rewards can seem harmless, they may skew recommendations toward policies that maximize the representative's benefits rather than meeting your needs.

For instance, you may be sold a policy loaded with unnecessary riders or inflated premiums, not because it's best for you, but because it helps the representative meet sales targets, unlock higher commission tiers, or qualify for performance-based bonuses. To avoid falling into this trap, this book provides actionable steps for evaluating the legitimacy of an insurance sales agent or broker and determining whether their motivations align with your goals.

The Problem with Being Sold to Instead of Empowered

At its core, the life insurance industry operates on a sales-driven model. Policies are sold, not chosen, and the consequences of this approach can be significant. Many consumers walk away from the purchasing process feeling overwhelmed and unsure of whether their policy is truly the best fit. Or worse, they have complete confidence that the wrong decision will best protect their family.

This book aims to flip the script by shifting the focus from being sold to being empowered. You'll learn how to take charge of your decisions by:

- **Understanding Your Goals:** Before exploring any policy, it's crucial to identify your financial objectives. Are you looking for basic coverage to protect your family, or do you need a policy that integrates with retirement planning?
- **Knowing What to Ask:** Agents and brokers may not volunteer information that doesn't serve their sales goals. By asking targeted questions—such as the long-term costs of a policy, the impact of riders, or the availability of alternatives—you can uncover obscured details that influence your decision.
- **Recognizing Red Flags:** Pressure-based sales tactics, vague explanations, or an overemphasis on complex features can be warning signs that you're being sold a policy rather than guided to the best option.

A Promise of Transparency

This book is built on a simple but important promise: to bring clarity and honesty to a life insurance sales industry that often leaves consumers in the dark. We'll walk you through the critical elements that many agents, brokers, and even financial advisors gloss over, not because they're unimportant, but because they don't serve the sales narrative. You deserve the full picture.

Here's what we'll uncover together:

The Influence of Commissions and Sales Incentives

We'll break down how compensation structures and sales goals often shape the recommendations you're given, and how you can recognize when a policy is being sold to benefit the agent or broker more than you. Understanding these dynamics is the first step toward putting your interests first.

The Complexity of Policy Design

Many life insurance policies today, including basic term policies, have become increasingly complex and often include optional riders and added benefits. Cash value policies, in particular, are frequently presented in overly simplified terms that do not accurately reflect the details outlined in the policy illustrations or contracts. While sales professionals are skilled at making complex products sound simple and appealing, the fine print often tells a very different story. This is why we strongly recommend that every policyholder seek a second, independent opinion before making any commitment.

Hidden Incentives Behind the Sale

From recruiting bonuses to sales contests and production-based rewards, many behind-the-scenes incentives can influence what's being recommended to you. We'll help you identify these hidden motivators and explain how they can impact the advice you receive.

By exposing what often goes unsaid, this book will equip you with the insight and tools to make informed, confident decisions, and ensure that your life insurance strategy is built around your needs, not someone else's agenda.

Life Insurance: A Tool, Not a Trap

Ultimately, life insurance is a powerful tool for financial security, when it's chosen wisely. It's not just about the death benefit; a well-structured policy can provide living benefits, cash value accumulation, tax advantages, and peace of mind. However, the industry's sales-driven structure often turns this tool into a trap, locking consumers into policies that don't align with their needs.

This book is your guide to breaking free from that trap. By prioritizing transparency, empowering you with knowledge, and offering actionable strategies, you can approach the life insurance process with confidence and clarity.

The Conflict of Ignorance: What Your Agents and Brokers Might Not Know

You may be thinking, my insurance guy is a friend of mine, I see him with his family around town, this guy would never take advantage of me. I get it. And so do the insurance companies. They know someone in your community, that you know, automatically has more of your trust. And we are not saying that your agent or broker is actively trying to do you harm.

While it's tempting to assume that agent or broker always prioritize their commissions over your best interests, the reality is often more nuanced. Many agents aren't trying to mislead you, they simply don't know any better. This conflict of ignorance stems from systemic issues within the industry that prioritize sales over education and foster environments where agent or broker are incentivized to remain uninformed about the broader market.

Drinking the Company Kool-Aid

Most agents start their careers with minimal training and experience. Their initial education often revolves around promoting and selling the products of the company they represent. These agents are taught to believe that their company's offerings are the best in the market, regardless of whether this is objectively true; especially whether it is true for you and your particular needs. They may not be exposed to alternative policies or strategies. Even if they are, there's little incentive for them to explore those options further.

In essence, agents are conditioned to "drink the Kool-Aid" of their employer or the marketing organization they associate with, accepting their promotions as gospel truth. This can lead to a cycle where agents unknowingly mislead clients, not out of malice but because they genuinely believe they're offering the best possible solution.

Ignorance Is Incentivized

Why don't agents seek out more knowledge about the wider array of life insurance products? Simply put, it's not in their best interest to do so. Here's why:

- **Commission Structures:** Agents and brokers are rewarded for selling specific products, often those with the highest premiums or additional features. Expanding their knowledge might lead them to recommend policies that offer less commission, which directly impacts their income.
- **Company Loyalty:** Captive agents—those who work for a single insurance company—are typically prohibited from selling policies outside their employer's portfolio. Learning about competing options could create professional frustration, as they'd be unable to act on that knowledge.
- **Overconfidence in Limited Expertise:** Early in their careers, agents may develop confidence based on limited training. This can lead to a dangerous combination of ignorance and overconfidence, where they genuinely believe their recommendations are the best available.

The Real Impact on Consumers

This systemic ignorance within the life insurance industry can have far-reaching consequences for consumers. One of the most significant issues is missed opportunities. When agents and brokers lack a comprehensive understanding of the available options, clients may never be introduced to policies that could offer better coverage, lower premiums, or greater flexibility. Without access to the full range of possibilities, consumers are often left settling for less than they deserve.

Another major concern is misaligned policies. For instance, an agents and brokers might push a high-cost permanent policy when a simple, more affordable term policy would have been the better fit. This misalignment not only leads to unnecessary complexity but also risks leaving clients overinsured or underinsured.

Lastly, ignorance can result in unnecessary costs. Consumers may find themselves paying for features or riders that don't serve their needs, simply because their agents and brokers wasn't aware of more tailored or cost-effective alternatives. Over time, these extra costs can add up, diminishing the overall value of the policy.

By failing to explore, compare, and verify options, agents and brokers inadvertently pass these burdens onto their clients, making it even more crucial for consumers to take an active role in their life insurance decisions.

How to Use This Book

This book is designed to bridge the knowledge gap, providing you with insights from my perspective as an expert life insurance planner and life insurance analyst. I have enlisted the help of my business partner, Attorney James Burns, to add his perspective on the legal complexities of the life insurance industry. Together, we offer a balanced, objective guide to help you make informed decisions.

Here's how each chapter is structured to empower you:

Expert Insights: Each chapter begins with an analysis of a critical aspect of life insurance, highlighting industry insights and breaking down complex topics into easy-to-understand concepts. You'll gain clarity on how the industry works and the strategies agents and brokers use to sell policies.

Actionable Strategies: Practical guidance is provided to help you identify your specific needs, compare policies, and ask the right questions. Whether you're new to life insurance or looking to review an existing policy, these strategies will help you stay in control of the process.

Workbook Features: To ensure this book is as useful as possible, each chapter includes interactive elements to guide your decision-making process. You'll find:

- Charts and infographics about the basics of life insurance planning.
- Checklists to evaluate policies and identify red flags.
- Worksheets to map out your financial goals and insurance needs.
- An Appendix with twelve case studies to illustrate the importance of review and working with an independent fiduciary professional.

Taking Control of Your Financial Future

By using this book as both a guide and a workbook, you'll be equipped to navigate the life insurance process with confidence. You'll learn how to:

- **Evaluate Your Needs:** Identify the type and amount of coverage that aligns with your goals.
- **Ask Better Questions:** Gain the knowledge needed to challenge agents and brokers, ensuring their recommendations align with your best interests.
- **Seek Independent Reviews:** Understand the value of unbiased second opinions, whether from fiduciary advisors or organizations like LifeInsuranceReview.com.

This book isn't just about buying life insurance, it's about empowering you to take control of your financial future. By the end of your journey, you'll not only understand the life insurance industry but also have the tools to make decisions that protect your family and build long-term financial security.

Let Me Introduce Myself:

I have been sharing a lot of knowledge with you without even introducing myself. I am John Nguyen, and together with James Burns, we are the brains behind LifeInsuranceReview.com (LIR). Our company's mission is to help people make informed and confident decisions about life insurance. Our company is positioned to be advocates for the consumer.

I want this book to be a resource to offer clarity in an industry often clouded by sales tactics and conflicts of interest. By combining decades of expertise, we've worked tirelessly to build a platform rooted in trust and transparency.

James, our entire advocate leadership team, and I each bring a unique perspective shaped by our personal and professional journeys. Our shared passion is empowering consumers in an industry where too many decisions are made for you, not by you.

This will be explained in detail in the next chapter, but it is imperative for you to understand this glaring point that makes us different. We and our team are fiduciaries. That means that we are legally bound to represent your best interests. Your life insurance sales agent probably can't say that.

More About Me

I've spent over two decades in the life insurance and financial planning industry, and what I've seen over those years has been both eye-opening and frustrating. When I first obtained my life insurance license in 2005, I was eager to help my family and others close to me secure their financial futures. But I quickly realized that the system wasn't built for the consumer, but to sell to consumers and to be as profitable as possible.

Independent agents like me who were recruited by a big insurance financial services company were trained to push certain products—not because they were the best fit for clients, but because they were the most profitable for the company. And the worst part? Most of us didn't even know much about what we were promoting and selling to our family and friends. We were taught to believe that our company's products were the best options for our clients. We were not encouraged, and often were discouraged, from exploring other options that were available in the marketplace.

I wanted to create a resource that does what most agents and brokers can't or won't do: put the consumer first and at the center of their business model. For me, it's not just about reviewing policies—it's about empowering the consumer to understand their life insurance needs and have access to a trusted independent resource, so people can make decisions based on unbiased information, not pressure.

Gaining a client's trust is something I take seriously because I know how rare transparency is in this sales-driven life insurance industry. I want every family we serve to walk away feeling confident, not confused or manipulated. That's what drives me every day.

From James Burns, my business partner: Bringing Legal Ethics to Financial Protection

As an estate planning attorney since 2000 and life insurance licensed since 2003, I've spent my career helping families and businesses protect their wealth and secure their legacies. Over the years, I've also seen firsthand how life insurance can be a powerful tool—when it's done right.

Unfortunately, I've also seen what happens when it's done wrong. Families who thought they had adequate protection find out too late that their policies don't deliver what they were promised. And more often than not, this isn't because their agent was trying to deceive them, it's because the agent didn't fully understand the product they were selling.

My background in law taught me the importance of fiduciary responsibility, putting the client's best interests above all else. But in the life insurance world, that's not the standard.

Through this platform with John, I've made it my mission to bring legal ethics to an industry that desperately needs them. I want to help people cut through the noise, understand the fine print, and make choices that truly protect their families. Trust is everything to me, and it's something we work hard to earn every day.

Overcoming Industry Challenges

Building LIR wasn't easy, as our firm stands on the opposite side of the life insurance sales industry. However, the need is there, as the life insurance sales industry has a low barrier to entry, and as many as 80% of new agents leave within their first year alone, leaving many who purchased a policy from them without a trusted advisor for support. This creates a landscape where most consumers purchase policies that are not the best option for them, leaving them short-changed on the back end.

Our firm is not just about pointing out flaws in the life insurance sales industry—it is about actively creating solutions that put consumers first. This conviction fueled our efforts, even when it meant going against the grain.

The motivation came from the tangible difference our work was making. Each time we served a client, secured the right policy, or avoided an expensive mistake, it reaffirmed our commitment to this mission. These victories, however small, remind us of the importance of what we are building.

Why This Matters to You

The "why" behind LIR is personal. I've seen too many families struggle because they didn't have the right information or support. We created this platform to change that.

Every review, every blog we post on our website, and every resource we provide is designed with you in mind. Our goal is to demystify the life insurance sales industry, help you understand your options, and empower you to make decisions that align with your goals, not someone else's commission and sales incentive structure.

Through the combined expertise of our entire LIR team, we offer a unique solution that bridges the gap between consumers and the life insurance industry. Our goal is to empower individuals to get the maximum value and benefit from the life insurance policies they want to own or already have in place.

Let this book be your guide, not just to understanding life insurance but to taking control of your financial future. You'll find insights that challenge the status quo, practical tools to evaluate your needs, and a roadmap to making choices with confidence.

We're here to empower you—not to sell to you. That's the LIR promise.

CHAPTER ONE

WHY FIDUCIARIES MATTER:

Guardians of Your Financial Future

The primary responsibility of fiduciaries is to run the plan solely in the interest of participants and beneficiaries and for the exclusive purpose of providing benefits and paying plan expenses. Fiduciaries must act prudently and minimize the risk.

– US Department of Labor

Understanding Fiduciaries and Their Critical Role

I have talked plenty about the compromised loyalties of the life insurance sales industry. When the weight of a multi-billion dollar industry is stacked against you, do you even have a chance? The answer is yes, and I will explain how.

The answer is: having fiduciaries on your side. A fiduciary isn't just another advisor; they are legally bound to act in your best interest, prioritizing your goals above their own.

In this chapter, I'll explore what a fiduciary is, why fiduciary-based guidance is vital in life insurance planning, and the levels of fiduciary roles you might encounter. I'll also examine the stark contrast between fiduciary professionals and traditional agents and brokers, highlighting the pitfalls of limited training, company affiliations, and the "conflict of ignorance."

What Is a Fiduciary?

A fiduciary is a financial professional who is legally and ethically required to act in your best interest. Unlike traditional agents or brokers, who may be influenced by their employer, marketing affiliations, or commission-based compensation structures, a fiduciary's primary responsibility is to serve you. This important distinction creates a more transparent, objective, and trustworthy relationship that is centered on your needs, not the advisor's financial incentives.

No, fiduciary is not necessarily a job title. Rather, it is a role that is included in certain professions, designations, or positions. You probably have encountered people acting in a fiduciary capacity at various points throughout your life. Examples include attorneys representing clients, guardians for minors, trustees managing trusts, executors of wills, certain financial advisors, board members of companies, healthcare agents, and real estate agents managing property on behalf of clients; essentially anyone who has a legal responsibility to act solely in the best interests of another person, putting the client's needs above their own in a situation requiring high levels of trust and loyalty.

So what can you expect from a fiduciary that you might not be getting from a commissioned salesperson? Fiduciary duty involves several key components:

- **Loyalty**: Fiduciaries must prioritize your goals and needs above their own financial interests.
- **Care**: A fiduciary is required to make recommendations based on a thorough understanding of your individual circumstances and what you want to accomplish.
- **Accountability**: Fiduciaries are held to a legal standard, meaning you have recourse if they fail to fulfill their duties.

This accountability is particularly important in life insurance because your policies can represent decades-long commitments. A fiduciary ensures that every decision is made with your best interests in mind.

The LIR Model of why a life Insurance review is essential:

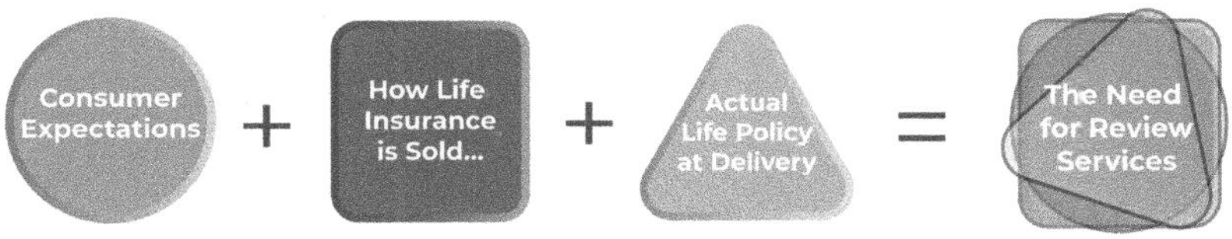

"This is a common issue, as consumers lack a trusted resource for LIFE INSURANCE REVIEW (LIR), especially when navigating the Free Look Period."

Why Fiduciary-Based Guidance Is Critical

The importance of choosing the right life insurance policy is real and should not be treated like a typical purchase. A poorly selected policy can leave your family underinsured, expose you to unnecessary costs, or tie you to features that don't match your long-term goals. Fiduciary-based guidance helps you avoid these pitfalls by focusing solely on what serves your best interests.

1. **Unbiased Recommendations**: Fiduciaries are not tied to specific companies or products, allowing them to provide a comprehensive view of the market.
2. **Clarity in Complexity**: Life insurance policies often include confusing terms and conditions. Fiduciaries take the time to break these down, ensuring you fully understand your choices.
3. **Empowerment Through Education**: A fiduciary serves as a guide in the decision-making process, equipping you with the knowledge needed to make informed, confident choices. Unlike many sales-driven professionals, fiduciaries do not steer you toward products that benefit them financially or limit your options to what they're allowed or incentivized to sell. Their focus is solely on what's best for you.

Levels of Fiduciary Guidance

Not all fiduciaries operate at the same level, and it's crucial to understand the distinctions when selecting a professional to guide you:

- **Fiduciary Agents**: Some agents claim to adhere to fiduciary principles but may still face limitations due to their employer's products. While they aim to act in your best interest, their recommendations can be constrained. So their fiduciary duty is limited to recommending the best of their offerings, not the best that is available to you.
- **Fiduciary Brokers**: Brokers generally have access to a broader range of products and may offer more impartial advice. However,

they often have contracts with specific insurers, which can create potential conflicts. They have the same caveat as above.

- **Fiduciary Financial Planners**: These professionals offer comprehensive financial guidance and help incorporate life insurance into your overall financial plan. However, many are not life insurance specialists and may lack in-depth knowledge of the wide range of products, policy designs, and options available in the marketplace. In some cases, they may also sell a limited selection of life insurance products, which can blur the line between truly objective advice and recommendations influenced by limited access or sales compensation.
- **Independent Analysts - Licensed Life Insurance Analyst**: These professionals represent the highest level of fiduciary guidance, providing unbiased reviews with no ties to specific insurers or any marketing companies.

The key to effective fiduciary guidance lies in independence and their depth of life insurance product and planning experience. A truly independent fiduciary has no financial incentive to recommend one product over another, ensuring that their advice is genuinely tailored to your needs. And that is the secret sauce to ensuring that your best interests are protected when buying life insurance.

Why Experience Matters

While fiduciary status sets a high ethical standard, experience is what ensures those standards translate into effective guidance. Inexperienced professionals, even those with good intentions, may lack the depth of knowledge needed to navigate the complexities of life insurance.

Experienced fiduciaries bring a wealth of knowledge to the table, including:

- **An Understanding of Policy Nuances**: From cash value components to term lengths and riders, experienced professionals know how to tailor policies to fit your unique needs.
- **Market Insight**: They can identify which providers offer the best options for specific situations.
- **Problem-Solving Skills**: Experience equips fiduciaries to anticipate and address potential issues, ensuring your policy continues to meet your goals over time.

When evaluating a fiduciary, always check their credentials, references, and track record. A seasoned professional will not only meet the fiduciary standard but also provide the expertise needed to guide you effectively.

The Realities of the Low Barrier to Entry

There are compelling reasons why an independent fiduciary is your best weapon in buying life insurance. Let's return, for a moment, to the analogy of buying a car. The process of buying a car is pretty straightforward. You know what you need, and with a little research, you can discover the information about the different cars that you are considering. You can explore the different models that fit your criteria. You can compare the relative merits (like gas mileage or cargo space) of the models you are considering against each other. Then you can verify your choice through a test drive.

I am the staunchest advocate of the explore, compare, and verify model to make the best choice for yourself. This is where the life insurance sales model falls short. First, you are too often given a limited set of choices. Second, life insurance is such a personal product and so much is hidden in the small print that it is almost impossible to get an apples-to-apples comparison to see what is best for you. Third, the only form of verification most consumers receive is when their sales agent pats them on the back and tells them what a great decision they have made. Not very reassuring...

One of the challenges in the life insurance industry that creates this scenario is its low barrier to entry. Becoming a licensed agent often requires minimal training, focusing more on sales techniques than on developing a comprehensive understanding of policies or financial planning. In fact, even someone who has no insurance or financial knowledge or experience can obtain a life insurance license within a week.

This creates a landscape where many agents are ill-equipped to provide meaningful guidance. Instead, they rely on prepackaged training from their employer, which often emphasizes specific products or sales tactics.

Plus, the first thing that new agents are encouraged to do is use their personal contacts to make their sales. Why would companies encourage this? Because there is a built-in trust factor with someone you know. Most of us believe that our friends and family have our best interests at heart. (And hopefully they do!). However, they may only know what their company has taught them.

The Conflict of Ignorance

While some agents may intentionally push high-commission products, many genuinely believe they are offering the best solutions. This "conflict of ignorance" stems from systemic issues within the industry.

New agents are often trained to focus on a limited set of products, with little exposure to the broader market. They are taught to believe in the superiority of their company's offerings, even if those products are not the best fit for every client.

This isn't malicious—it's a byproduct of a system that prioritizes sales over service. However, the consequences for consumers can be significant:

- **Overpaying for Policies**: Clients may end up with expensive policies that don't provide adequate coverage.
- **Unnecessary Features**: Riders and add-ons may be included simply to increase premiums.
- **Better Fit for Your Needs**: Without access to the full market, agents can't identify policies that offer better value or flexibility.

This is where an independent fiduciary is vital for your protection. A fiduciary's independence and experience eliminate this conflict, ensuring that every recommendation is made with your goals in mind.

A Fiduciary's Role in Empowering You

Ultimately, a fiduciary isn't just a guide, they're a partner in your financial journey. By prioritizing your interests, providing clear explanations, and empowering you with knowledge, fiduciaries transform the life insurance process from a stressful transaction into a confident decision. You can go from believing to knowing.

When you work with a fiduciary, you gain:

- **Clarity**: A clear understanding of your options and how they align with your goals.
- **Confidence**: The assurance that every recommendation is made with your best interest in mind.
- **Control**: The ability to make informed decisions without pressure or confusion.

Essentially, you can explore, compare, and verify easily. The peace of mind that comes from fiduciary-based guidance is invaluable, so your life insurance policy truly protects your loved ones and supports your long-term financial goals.

The Importance of Certifications in Evaluating Life Insurance

On the life insurance search, you will encounter an alphabet soup of letters. We wanted to give you a quick reference guide for what these letters represent and what they mean to you. When evaluating life insurance, certifications are a key indicator of a professional's expertise and commitment to their craft. While a basic license allows someone to sell life insurance, certifications demonstrate a deeper understanding of the industry and its complexities. Certifications also represent extensive studying and testing. Here are the most notable designations to consider when selecting a professional:

CLU® (Chartered Life Underwriter)

The CLU designation is the gold standard in life insurance. Established in 1927, it represents a comprehensive mastery of life insurance products, advanced client servicing techniques, and an in-depth understanding of financial protection strategies. Achieving this certification requires extensive study and is considered the most difficult designation for life insurance professionals to obtain, showcasing a level of dedication and expertise that goes beyond the minimum requirements.

ChFC® (Chartered Financial Consultant)

For those seeking financial planning that integrates insurance into a broader strategy, the ChFC designation is ideal. This certification emphasizes comprehensive financial planning that integrates life insurance, annuities, long-term care, and disability products. Professionals with this designation are well-equipped to align your life insurance needs with your long-term financial goals.

CFP® (Certified Financial Planner)

The CFP is widely regarded as the pinnacle of financial planning certifications. Known for its rigorous standards, it is also fiduciary-based, meaning CFP professionals are legally obligated to act in your best interest. This credential reflects a holistic approach to financial advice, making it highly relevant when life insurance is part of a broader financial strategy.

Life Insurance Analyst

This license holds a prestigious distinction, and is recognized by the many applicable State's Department of Insurance including New York and California. The Life Insurance Analyst license was created in 1941, a credential only held by fewer than 1% of life insurance professionals. For further exclusivity, an even smaller percentage of agencies hold this license at the entity level.

Remember, not all credentials carry equal weight. Some certifications are primarily marketing tools rather than rigorous demonstrations of expertise. Understanding the significance of a designation helps you discern the truly qualified professionals from those leveraging less meaningful titles.

Certifications can help you understand whether you're working with individuals who have the knowledge to guide you through the complexities of life insurance, from tax implications to investment components, and provide the best possible advice tailored to your needs.

Experience Matters: Expertise Beyond Sales

As we've explored, fiduciary-based guidance is essential because it ensures your interests come first. But even among fiduciaries, experience plays a critical role in delivering advice that genuinely protects and empowers you. The life insurance industry's low barriers to entry mean many agents start with limited knowledge, leaving consumers vulnerable to poorly tailored recommendations.

This lack of expertise is compounded by the complexity of life insurance products. Policies often include intricate terms, varying premium structures, and optional riders that can confuse even seasoned professionals. An experienced fiduciary can cut through the noise, helping you focus on what matters most to your unique circumstances.

When working with a fiduciary, take the time to ask about their experience and qualifications. For example, have they worked with clients who have similar needs to yours? Do they hold certifications like CLU® or ChFC® that demonstrate advanced expertise? These factors can make the difference between sound guidance and costly mistakes.

The Emotional Toll of the Sales Process

As we have discussed, the traditional life insurance sales process is often designed to work against you. Nobody wants to think about death. Agents know that emotions run high when discussing topics like death, family protection, and long-term security. They leverage this vulnerability to create a sense of urgency, pressuring you into decisions before you're ready.

For many consumers, the process feels overwhelming. Here are some signs that you need someone on your side to protect your interests:

Confusion: Dense policy language and technical jargon leave you unsure about what you're buying.

Fatigue: Long meetings filled with information you don't fully understand can wear you down.

Stress: The gravity of protecting your loved ones creates emotional pressure that's difficult to manage.

Don't fool yourself into thinking you are the only person feeling this way. These tactics aren't accidental, they're designed to make you more likely to agree to a policy. Luckily, fiduciaries approach the process differently. Instead of rushing you into a decision, they create a space where you feel informed, respected, and supported.

Advice vs. Counsel: What Sets Fiduciaries Apart

One of the most significant benefits of working with a fiduciary is the distinction between advice and counsel. Traditional agents and brokers are often focused on selling, which shapes the recommendations they provide. Their advice tends to center on the products they're incentivized to promote, and whether or not those products align with your needs.

Fiduciaries, on the other hand, offer counsel. This means they act as a partner in your decision-making process, prioritizing your goals and helping you navigate your options.

The difference isn't just ethical—it's practical. Counsel ensures that:

Your goals drive the conversation: Recommendations are based on your needs, not a sales quota.

You have options: Fiduciaries present a range of policies, explaining the pros and cons of each.

You remain in control: Every decision is yours to make, free from pressure or manipulation.

Empowering You to Decide

At its core, fiduciary guidance is about empowerment. When you're educated and informed, you're no longer at the mercy of pressure-based sales tactics. Instead, you're equipped to make decisions that reflect your priorities.

Fiduciaries achieve this by:

Educating You: They break down complex policies into plain language, ensuring you understand every aspect of your coverage.

Providing Perspective: Fiduciaries help you see how life insurance fits into your broader financial strategy, from protecting loved ones to building wealth.

Respecting Your Role: They recognize that the ultimate decision belongs to you, supporting rather than directing your choices.

This empowerment is transformative. Instead of feeling overwhelmed by the process, you'll approach life insurance with confidence and clarity.

Built-In Protections and Guardrails

Even within a sales-driven industry, there are consumer protections designed to safeguard your interests. Fiduciaries ensure these protections are fully utilized, acting as an additional layer of security.

Key guardrails include:

- **Free Look Periods:** Most policies allow you to cancel within a specified timeframe—typically 10 to 30 days (it varies by state)—without penalty. This gives you time to calmly reconsider your decision and seek a second opinion, which you definitely should. There is more information on this in Chapter Seven of this book.

- **Senior Protections:** Additional rules ensure older consumers are not subjected to undue pressure or misleading tactics, and to encourage them to thoroughly review their final policies.
- **Marketing Regulations:** Policies must be presented transparently with clear disclosures, reducing the risk of deceptive claims.

These protections are valuable, but they're only effective if you're aware of them. Too often salespeople, eager to close the deal, gloss over these protections. A fiduciary ensures that you understand your rights and have the tools to protect yourself.

Commission-Based Sales vs. Fiduciary Guidance - Perspective from James

James Burns explains the differences between fiduciary advisors and traditional life insurance agents like this:

"The difference is night and day. Fiduciaries have no financial incentive to push one policy over another. Our goal is to find the best solution for you, not the most profitable option for us."

In contrast, traditional agents often work on commission, earning a percentage of the premiums from the policies they sell. This creates inherent conflicts of interest, where the agent's priorities may not align with yours. Additional incentives, like bonuses, trips, and awards, further skew their recommendations.

A fiduciary eliminates these conflicts by focusing solely on your needs. This transparency fosters trust, ensuring that every recommendation is made with your best interests in mind.

Stories of Fiduciary Success - Reference Appendix for Case Studies

I have seen countless examples of consumers being misled by traditional agents. One client came to me with a complex indexed universal life policy loaded with high policy charges and expenses, unnecessary riders, resulting in premiums they could barely afford just three years later.

After reviewing their needs, it was clear this policy didn't align with their needs and financial planning goals. I recommended a simpler, more affordable term policy that provided better value and protection. It wasn't just about saving money, it was about giving them peace of mind.

By exploring, comparing, and verifying options, fiduciaries ensure that you're not locked into policies that benefit the salesperson more than you.

The Explore, Compare, Verify Process

At LIR, we've built our process around empowering consumers through unbiased, conflict-free guidance. This three-step approach ensures that every decision is made with clarity and confidence:

Explore: We offer a comprehensive view of the life insurance marketplace, helping you understand the full spectrum of options that best align with your needs. This includes guiding you through fixed, indexed, dividend-paying, and variable products, so you can make informed comparisons with confidence.

Compare: Our independent reviews clearly outline the strengths and limitations of each option, helping you confidently determine which policy best aligns with your goals and needs.

Verify: We thoroughly assess each recommendation to ensure it aligns with your specific needs, financial goals, budget, and long-term strategy. This includes verifying that the product structure, features, and costs are appropriate for your situation, not just now, but well into the future. Our process provides an added layer of protection, helping you avoid mismatched policies and ensuring you make decisions with clarity and confidence.

About 90% of the policies that we review can be improved. NINETY PERCENT! If you wonder why we are passionate about the benefit of fiduciary review, there is your answer. These are all good-intentioned people who want to make the best choices for their family or business after they are gone, completely stymied by the life insurance sales machine.

We know our duties as independent fiduciaries, to protect your best interest. It is sad that the life insurance sales industry is not held to the same standard.

CHAPTER TWO

THE DIFFERENT TYPES OF LIFE INSURANCE EXPLAINED

A man who dies without adequate life insurance should have to come back and see the mess he created.

— Will Rogers

A Primer on the Major Types of Life Insurance Policies

Life insurance is a versatile tool that can protect your family, provide financial security, and if designed properly, serve as a cornerstone for building long term wealth. Understanding the different types of policies is the first step in selecting the one that fits your needs. This section provides a comprehensive overview of the four major types of life insurance products: term life insurance, whole life insurance, universal life insurance, and variable life insurance. Use this as a reference to help you understand the purpose and functionality of each policy type.

It's important to understand that many additional benefits and enhancements are available through specific products, beyond what is covered in this discussion of policy types.

1. Term Life Insurance

Overview

Term life insurance is the simplest and most affordable type of life insurance. It provides coverage for a specific time frame, such as 10, 20, or 30 years. If you pass away during the policy term, the insurer pays the death benefit to your beneficiaries. Once the term ends, the policy expires unless it is renewed, converted to permanent coverage, or replaced with a new policy.

Key Features

- **Affordable Premiums**: Term life policies are typically less expensive than permanent policies because they focus solely on coverage without accumulating cash value.
- **Fixed Coverage Period**: You select the term length, making it an ideal option for temporary needs like paying off a mortgage or funding your children's education.
- **Straightforward Terms**: There are no additional investment components, which makes term policies easy to understand and manage.

Who It's For

Term life insurance is an excellent choice for individuals or families who need coverage for a specific period. It's particularly suitable for younger families, new homeowners, or those with financial obligations they expect to outgrow.

Drawbacks

While term life insurance is affordable and effective for short-term needs, it comes with limitations:

- **No Cash Value**: If the policyholder outlives the term, there's no return on premiums *unless* the policy includes a return-of-premium rider.
- **Rising Renewal Costs**: Renewing a policy after the initial term can be costly due to increased age and potential health concerns.

Term life insurance is a cost-effective way to secure peace of mind during key periods of your life. However, it's important to review your evolving needs periodically to ensure that you still have adequate coverage for your changing needs.

2. Whole Life Insurance

Overview

Whole life insurance provides lifelong coverage, as long as premiums are paid. Unlike term life insurance, it includes a cash value component that grows at a guaranteed rate over time. This makes whole life insurance a dual-purpose product: it offers financial protection and acts as a savings vehicle.

Key Features

- **Lifetime Protection**: The policy remains in force throughout the insured's lifetime, ensuring beneficiaries receive the death benefit regardless of when the insured passes away.

- **Cash Value Accumulation**: A portion of your premiums goes into a cash value account that grows at a guaranteed rate. This cash value can be borrowed against or withdrawn if needed.
- **Fixed Costs of Insurance and Premiums**: Premiums normally remain consistent over the life of the policy, offering predictability.

Who It's For

Whole life insurance is a strong choice for individuals seeking long-term coverage with the added benefit of cash value accumulation. It's particularly useful for estate planning, creating a guaranteed inheritance, or covering final expenses.

Drawbacks

Whole life insurance can be more expensive than other types of policies due to its permanent coverage and cash value features. Additionally, while the cash value grows at a guaranteed rate, it typically earns *less* than market-based investments.

For individuals with significant financial assets or estate planning needs, whole life insurance provides stability and long-term value. Its simplicity and predictability make it a reliable option for securing a legacy or managing future financial needs.

3. Universal Life Insurance

Overview

Universal life insurance offers the flexibility of adjustable premiums and death benefits while maintaining a cash value component. Unlike whole life insurance, which is more rigid in its structure, universal life policies allow policyholders to modify their payments and coverage as their financial needs change.

Key Features

- **Adjustable Premiums**: Policyholders can increase, decrease, or even skip premiums, provided the cash value is sufficient to cover policy costs.
- **Flexible Death Benefit**: The death benefit can be adjusted up or down within the limits of the policy, making it adaptable to changing circumstances.
- **Cash Value Growth**: The cash value grows based on current interest rates or market performance, depending on the type of universal life policy.

Types of Universal Life Insurance

1. **Traditional Universal Life (UL)**: Cash value growth is tied to prevailing interest rates, which are determined by the insurer.
2. **Indexed Universal Life (IUL)**: The cash value's growth is *linked to a market index*, such as the S&P 500. IUL policies offer potential for higher returns with a minimum guaranteed interest rate to protect against market downturns.
3. **Guaranteed Universal Life (GUL):** The primary objective is to guarantee the death benefit for as long as you live, not to accumulate cash value.
4. **Variable Universal Life (VUL)**: Allows policyholders to invest the cash value in sub-accounts similar to mutual funds, offering greater growth potential but also more risk.

Who It's For

Universal life insurance is ideal for individuals seeking flexibility in their life insurance coverage. It's particularly appealing to those with fluctuating income or changing financial goals. Indexed Universal Life (IUL), for instance, is well-suited for individuals interested in *combining protection with market-linked growth* opportunities.

Drawbacks

- **Complexity**: Universal life policies require active management to ensure the cash value remains sufficient to cover costs.
- **Market Risks**: IUL and VUL policies are subject to market fluctuations, which can impact cash value and coverage.

Universal life insurance provides adaptability and the potential for cash value growth, making it a versatile option for long-term financial planning. However, it's important to work with an experienced advisor to navigate its complexities.

4. Variable Life Insurance

Overview

Variable life insurance combines permanent coverage with investment opportunities. Policyholders can allocate their cash value among various sub-accounts, similar to mutual funds, giving them control over how their money is invested.

Key Features

- **Investment Opportunities**: Policyholders can choose from a range of sub-accounts, influencing the growth of their cash value.

- **Tax Advantages**: Investment growth is tax-deferred, and the death benefit is generally tax-free to beneficiaries.
- **Death Benefit Variability**: The death benefit may increase or decrease based on the performance of the investments.

Who It's For

Variable life insurance appeals to individuals with higher risk tolerance who are comfortable with market volatility. It's a good fit for those seeking to integrate life insurance with long-term investment strategies.

Drawbacks

- **Market Risks**: Poor investment performance can erode the cash value and reduce the death benefit.
- **Fees and Costs**: Management fees, policy charges, and sub-account expenses can significantly impact returns.

While variable life insurance offers the potential for significant growth, it requires careful management and a willingness to accept market risks. For those with financial savvy or access to a trusted advisor, it can be a powerful tool for wealth accumulation.

Comparing the Policies

Here is a quick chart to compare the features of the general different types of policies. Understanding how these policies compare helps clarify which one aligns best with your needs:

Feature	Term Life	Whole Life	Universal Life	Variable Life
Coverage Duration	Specific Term	Lifetime	Lifetime (Adjustable)	Lifetime
Premiums	Low	High	Flexible	Flexible
Cash Value	None	Insurance Company Dividends	Market/Index Linked	Investment Sub-Accounts
Investment Options	None	None	Limited (Index/Market)	Broad Sub-Accounts
Risk	Low	Low	Moderate	High

Choosing the Right Policy

Selecting the right type of life insurance depends on your financial goals, risk tolerance, and coverage needs. Here's a quick summary:

- **Choose Term Life** if you need affordable, high-value coverage for a temporary period.
- **Choose Whole Life** if you want lifelong coverage with guaranteed and more predictable cash value growth.
- **Choose Universal Life** if you need flexibility in premiums and death benefits.
- **Choose Variable Life** if you're comfortable with investment risks and want to maximize growth potential.

Understanding these options will help you choose a policy that aligns with your priorities, or at least give you a solid starting point for a conversation with any life insurance professional. Remember, life insurance is more than just a safety net, it's a powerful tool for building a secure financial future.

Understanding Life Insurance as an Asset

Life insurance is not just a safety net for your loved ones; it can also be a powerful financial asset. When chosen and managed wisely, the right life insurance policy can provide living benefits, serve as a wealth-building tool, and offer flexibility for evolving needs. Yet, too often, consumers may be misdirected by sales tactics, resulting in policies that might not align with their goals.

A Living Asset

Life insurance is traditionally associated with death benefits, but many policies include **living benefits** that allow you to access funds while you're still alive. These can be used for critical illnesses, long-term care, or even supplementing retirement income. Understanding these features is critical to maximizing the value of your policy.

Living Benefits in Action

Living benefits can include:

- **Accelerated Death Benefits**: Access to a portion of the death benefit in cases of disability, chronic, critical, and terminal illness.
- **Cash Value Access**: Permanent policies like whole life, universal life, and variable life allow you to borrow against or withdraw from the accumulated cash value.
- **Long-Term Care Riders**: Some policies include options to fund long-term care, reducing the need for separate insurance.

For example, a client had a whole life policy with significant cash value. When faced with unexpected financial hardship, they were able **to borrow against the policy** to cover costs without depleting their savings. This flexibility provided critical financial relief during a challenging time.

Empowerment vs. Salesmanship

We want you to understand the different types of insurance before you begin the buying process. Life insurance is generally a "high-touch" business. The considerations are deeply personal, and the process often involves discussing emotional topics like mortality and family protection. Unfortunately, this emotional connection can be exploited by sales-focused agents and brokers.

The Emotional Sale

Agents and brokers may use emotional triggers to push high-premium policies or unnecessary riders. For instance, they might stress the potential risks of being underinsured without explaining the costs and trade-offs of additional features.

Empowered Decision-Making

In contrast, we want you to understand your options, and respect your ability to decide what's best for your family and provide guidance without pressure. This includes:

- Explaining the benefits and limitations of each policy.
- Offering transparency about costs and potential risks.
- Helping you align your choices with your financial goals.

The Magic Show: Avoiding Misdirection

In the sales-driven world of life insurance, misdirection is a common tactic. (i.e. pay no mind to this small print, check out the amazing tax-free death benefit for your family). Life insurance sales professionals are no different, they may emphasize certain policy features while downplaying others, creating a "magic show" effect that distracts you from the specific details that matter.

Common Misdirection Tactics:

- Highlighting potential cash value growth without explaining associated fees or risks.
- Promoting riders that sound valuable but add little practical benefit for most consumers.
- Overemphasizing a policy's flexibility without clarifying the management responsibilities it requires.

How to Stay Focused

- **Ask Questions**: Don't be afraid to challenge vague explanations. Ask for specifics about costs, benefits, and risks.
- **Do Your Research**: Use resources like LifeInsuranceReview.com to explore unbiased reviews and insights.
- **Work With a Fiduciary**: A fiduciary will guide you through the process with transparency, ensuring you're not misled by flashy sales tactics.

Research and Choose Wisely

Selecting the right life insurance policy is one of the most important financial decisions you'll make. It's worth taking the time to research, ask questions, and evaluate your options. A policy that aligns with your goals can provide immense peace of mind, but the wrong choice can lead to unnecessary expenses or inadequate coverage.

Key steps to take:

1. **Assess Your Needs**: Determine what you want the policy to achieve—protection, wealth building, or estate planning.
2. **Compare Policies**: Understand the pros and cons of each type of insurance to find the best fit.
3. **Seek Expertise**: Consult with experienced fiduciaries who prioritize your interests over commissions.

By approaching life insurance with clarity, purpose, and the right information, you can turn it from a confusing product into a powerful financial tool that protects and supports your future needs and goals.

CHAPTER THREE

LIFE INSURANCE IS FANTASTIC

(But Only if it Meets YOUR Goals!)

Experts are experts, even when they are wrong.

– **Niels Bohr,** Danish theoretical physicist

I want to make it perfectly clear, I love what insurance can do. It's a powerful tool, and in most cases, it should absolutely be part of a well-rounded financial plan. But here's the truth: life insurance that doesn't match your specific needs, goals, and situation is like driving a two-seater sports car when what you really need is a reliable family SUV. Sure, it'll get you from point A to point B, but it won't serve your purpose, and you'll likely pay far more than necessary. My goal is to make sure that doesn't happen to you.

Life insurance is amazing! It is one of the most powerful financial tools available. When designed to meet your specific goals, it becomes more than just a safety net for your loved ones, it's a critical asset that provides security, flexibility, and peace of mind. This chapter explores the fundamental reasons why life insurance matters for families, business.

This chapter explains why life insurance is essential for anyone with financial responsibilities. It covers the key benefits a policy can provide and makes the case for why every individual needs coverage that is tailored to their specific needs and goals.

As Illustrated Below:

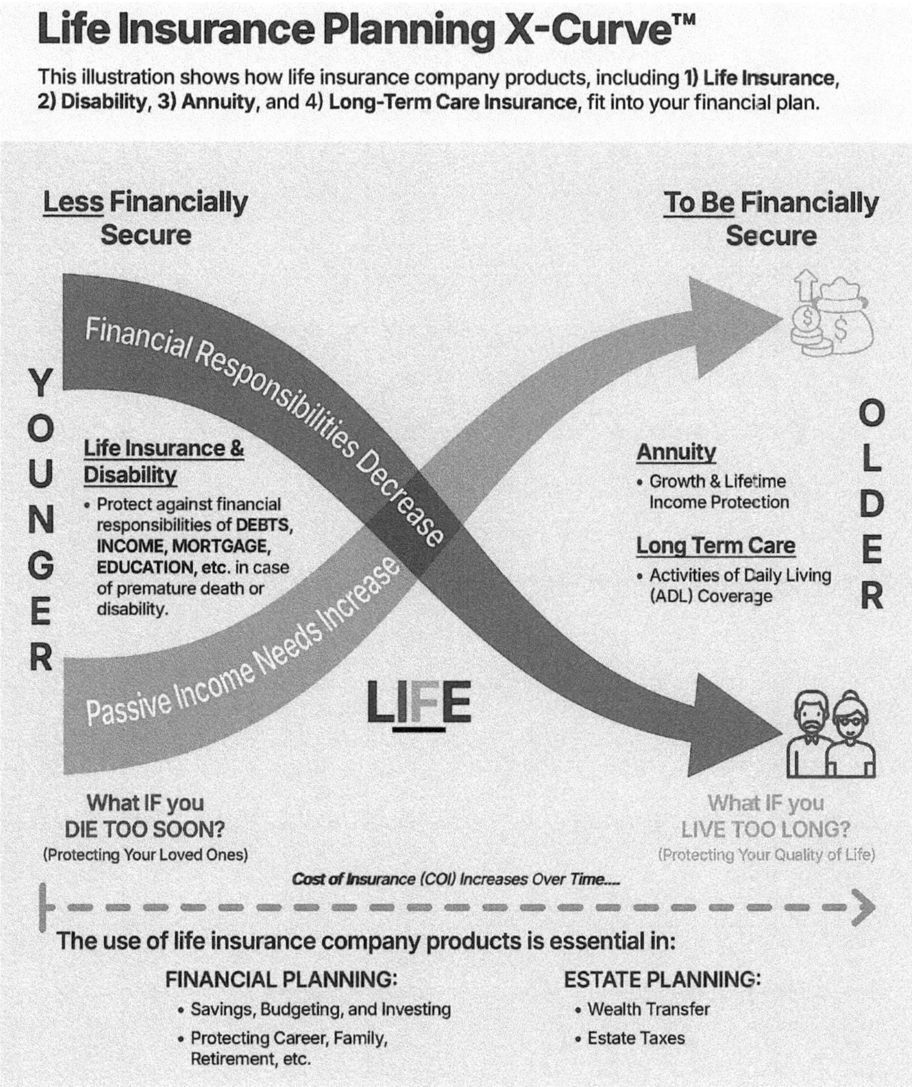

Why Life Insurance Is Important

At its core, life insurance is about protecting what matters most. Whether you're a parent, a business owner, or an individual planning for the future, a well-structured life insurance policy ensures that your financial goals are safeguarded against life's uncertainties.

1. For Families:

Families are often the primary beneficiaries of life insurance, and for good reason. In the event of an unexpected death, life insurance provides financial stability, helping families navigate one of the most challenging times in their lives.

- **Income Replacement:** Life insurance ensures that your family can maintain their standard of living by replacing lost income. This is especially critical if you are the primary breadwinner.
- **Debt Coverage:** A life insurance policy can pay off significant debts like a mortgage, car loans, or credit card balances, preventing your loved ones from inheriting financial burdens.
- **Education Costs:** For parents, life insurance can secure your children's future by funding college or other educational needs.

2. For Business Owners

For entrepreneurs and business owners, life insurance plays a vital role in ensuring business continuity and protecting the livelihoods of employees and partners.

- **Buy-Sell Agreements:** Life insurance funds buy-sell agreements, allowing remaining business partners to buy out the deceased owner's share and maintain control.

- **Key Person Insurance:** Policies on key employees or executives provide businesses with financial protection in the event of their untimely death.
- **Debt and Operating Expenses:** Business-focused life insurance ensures that debts or operational costs can be covered, keeping the business afloat during transitions.

3. For Individuals

Even for individuals without dependents, life insurance can be an important part of a financial plan.

- **Final Expenses:** Policies can cover funeral costs, medical bills, or other end-of-life expenses, ensuring these costs aren't left to family or friends.
- **Legacy Building:** Life insurance allows you to leave a financial gift to a charity, relative, or institution that reflects your values and priorities.
- **Tax-Advantaged Wealth Transfer**: For those with significant assets, life insurance can provide a tax-efficient way to transfer wealth to heirs.

Benefits of Life Insurance

Life insurance offers a range of benefits that extend beyond financial security. When properly aligned with your goals, these policies become versatile tools that support your long-term vision.

1. Financial Protection for Loved Ones

The most obvious benefit of life insurance is the financial security it provides to your beneficiaries. The death benefit can replace lost income, pay for major expenses, and offer a financial cushion during difficult times.

2. Wealth Building and Cash Value

Permanent policies like whole life and universal life accumulate cash value over time, which can be accessed through loans or withdrawals. This cash value grows tax-deferred, making it a valuable component of a comprehensive financial plan.

3. Flexibility Through Riders

Life insurance policies can be customized with riders, which are additional features or benefits. Examples include:

- **Accelerated Death Benefit Riders:** Allow access to a portion of the death benefit in the event of a disability, chronic, critical, or terminal illness.
- **Disability Waiver of Premium Riders**: Waive premiums if you become disabled and unable to work.
- **Long-Term Care Riders:** Provide funds for long-term care expenses if needed.

4. Tax Advantages

Life insurance policies come with significant tax benefits:

- **Tax-Free Death Benefit:** Beneficiaries typically receive the death benefit tax-free.
- **Tax-Deferred Growth:** The cash value in permanent policies grows without being subject to annual taxes.

- **Estate Tax Planning:** For high-net-worth individuals, life insurance can be structured to minimize estate taxes.

5. Peace of Mind

Perhaps the most underrated benefit of life insurance is the peace of mind it provides. Knowing that your family, business, or financial legacy is protected allows you to focus on living fully and pursuing your goals without constant worry.

Why You Need Life Insurance

Talking about life insurance can be uncomfortable because it forces us to consider a future without ourselves in it. While no one likes to dwell on that reality, the truth is none of us live forever. What many people don't realize is that life insurance isn't just about death, it offers living benefits that can provide financial support during your lifetime as well. Despite its many advantages, life insurance remains one of the most misunderstood and underutilized tools in personal financial planning. That's why it should be viewed not as a luxury, but as a necessity for almost everyone.

1. Life Is Unpredictable

No one knows what tomorrow will bring. Life insurance provides a financial safety net, ensuring that an untimely death doesn't lead to financial devastation for your loved ones.

2. Costs Are Manageable

Many people assume life insurance is expensive, but term policies can be highly affordable, especially for younger individuals in good health.

Permanent policies, while more expensive, offer additional benefits that justify the cost for many.

3. It's an Act of Love

Purchasing life insurance is one of the most selfless financial decisions you can make. It's a tangible way to show your loved ones that you care about their future, even when you're no longer there to provide for them.

4. Business Continuity Depends on It

For entrepreneurs, life insurance isn't just personal protection—it's a critical business tool. Without it, businesses may face significant financial strain, leading to closures or layoffs.

5. It's Adaptable to Your Needs

Life insurance isn't a one-size-fits-all product. Whether you're looking for affordable short-term coverage or a permanent policy with investment features, there's an option that fits your goals and budget.

Beware of the Emotional Sell

While life insurance is a fantastic financial product, the process of purchasing it may often be filled with misdirection. Life insurance sales professionals may highlight features like cash value growth or riders without fully explaining the costs or limitations. They also may present a policy as your "best option" when it is only the best among *their* offerings. Or they may flood you with facts and figures to confuse you. I call this the "magic show" effect. Beware, it can lead you to make decisions based on emotion rather than logic.

How to Make Sure You Aren't Sold

Ask Questions: Understand what you're buying and why it's recommended.

Clearly Understand Your Goals: The sales process is stacked against you, make sure you understand exactly what you want.

Work With a Fiduciary or a fiduciary organization like LIR: A fiduciary advisor prioritizes your goals over commissions.

Compare Options: Don't settle for the first policy offered—explore alternatives to find the best fit.

As with all things, empowerment comes from understanding your choices. By taking the time to research and consult with experts, you can get a policy that serves your unique goals.

Life insurance is not just a product, it's a plan for the people and priorities that matter most to you. Whether you're protecting a family, securing a business, or planning a legacy, the right policy can make all the difference.

If you haven't already, take the time to evaluate your needs, explore your options, and consult with a trusted advisor.

There Is No "Best" Policy, Only What's Best for You

It's important to remember when it comes to life insurance, there's no one-size-fits-all solution. The "best" policy isn't defined by industry awards or catchy advertisements, it's determined by how well it meets your specific needs and budget. What works for a young professional might not work for a family with children, and what suits a business owner's estate planning needs may be overkill for someone nearing retirement.

The key is understanding that life insurance isn't just about choosing a product, it's about designing a solution that provides the financial security and flexibility you and your loved ones require. This starts with evaluating your goals, knowing your financial responsibilities, and ensuring the policy is tailored to fit your circumstances.

Life Insurance Is a Guarantee—If Designed Properly

At its heart, life insurance is a promise: if something happens to you, your loved ones or business will have the financial resources they need. The life insurance industry, by and large, does a great job at this. But that guarantee only holds if the policy is structured correctly.

Properly designed life insurance does more than just provide a death benefit—it accounts for critical aspects of your financial life, including:

- **Adequate Coverage**: Ensuring the death benefit is sufficient to cover your family's expenses, debts, and long-term needs.
- **Cost Effectiveness**: Balancing coverage with affordability so the policy doesn't strain your current finances.
- **Flexibility**: Incorporating features or riders that align with your specific goals, such as living benefits or long-term care options.

Without careful planning, life insurance may fail to deliver on its promise. For example, policies that are too small might leave your family scrambling to make ends meet, while overly complicated plans can burden your budget with unnecessary features.

Protecting Your Family's Financial Future

The most common reason people purchase life insurance is to protect their families. A well-designed policy can provide peace of mind, ensuring your loved ones won't face financial hardship in your absence.

Critical Areas of Protection

- **Income Replacement**: Life insurance can replace your income, covering everyday expenses like rent, groceries, and childcare.
- **Education Funding**: Policies can set aside funds to ensure your children's educational goals are met.
- **Debt Repayment**: Life insurance can settle outstanding debts, such as a mortgage or car loan, so your family isn't burdened with these obligations.

I had a client whose spouse had passed away unexpectedly. The family relied on the deceased's income to cover their mortgage and other bills. However, the life insurance policy they had was insufficient. Within six months, the family had to sell their home and relocate. Even years later, this case sticks with me. It is a painful reminder of how important it is to ensure coverage truly meets the family's needs. It is also the motivation for this book. I don't want this to happen to you.

Estate Planning, Business Continuity, and Debt Repayment

Life insurance isn't just for individuals or families—it's also a powerful tool for estate planning and business continuity.

For Estate Planning

High-net-worth individuals often use life insurance to manage estate taxes and ensure a seamless transfer of wealth. By designating the policy to cover estate liabilities, heirs can avoid selling assets like property or businesses to pay taxes.

For Business Owners

Business continuity often depends on life insurance. Key person insurance ensures that the company can weather the loss of a vital employee or owner. Similarly, buy-sell agreements funded by life insurance enable surviving partners to buy out the deceased's share, maintaining control and stability.

Debt Repayment

Many people overlook how life insurance can be used to clear outstanding debts. Whether it's a mortgage, business loan, or personal debt, a policy can relieve your family or business of financial obligations they might not be equipped to handle.

Watch Out for Life Insurance as an Add-On

Life insurance is too important to be treated as an afterthought or bundled with unrelated products. Unfortunately, it's often sold as an add-on to other types of insurance, like home, auto, or even credit card protection.

Why This Is a Problem

- **Limited Coverage**: Bundled policies typically offer minimal coverage, far less than what most families or businesses require.

- **Lack of Customization**: These policies are often generic and fail to address your unique goals or needs.
- **High Costs**: When life insurance is packaged with other products, you may end up paying more than you would for a standalone policy with better features.

"Life insurance isn't a Swiss Army Knife," James explains. "It's a specialized tool that needs to be tailored to your situation. Treating it like an add-on devalues its importance and effectiveness."

Why a Second Opinion Matters

Even if you already have life insurance, it's worth getting a second opinion to ensure your policy aligns with your current needs. Over time, your financial situation, goals, and responsibilities change. A thorough review can identify gaps or inefficiencies in your coverage.

Common Findings During Reviews

- **Underinsured Policies**: Many people have less coverage than they need, leaving their families vulnerable.
- **Unnecessary Riders**: Policies may include features that add cost without providing meaningful benefits.
- **Missed Opportunities**: Some policies aren't optimized for cash value growth or tax efficiency.

At LifeInsuranceReview.com, we've helped countless clients improve their coverage through unbiased reviews. Whether it's recommending a policy conversion, identifying cost savings, or ensuring the death benefit aligns with their needs, our process empowers consumers to make informed decisions.

Common Misconceptions About Life Insurance - Perspective from James

Despite its importance, life insurance is often misunderstood. James addresses some of the most common myths:

- **"I'm Too Young to Need Life Insurance"**: In reality, purchasing life insurance when you're young and healthy is the most cost-effective time to do so. Rates are lower, and you're more likely to qualify for better terms.
- **"It's Too Expensive"**: Many people overestimate the cost of life insurance. Term policies, in particular, offer substantial coverage at affordable rates.
- **"I Don't Have Dependents"**: Even if you don't have children or a spouse, life insurance can cover debts, final expenses, and leave a legacy to a cause or organization you care about.
- **"My Employer Provides Life Insurance"**: Employer-sponsored policies often offer limited coverage and may not be portable if you change jobs.

James stresses the importance of breaking these misconceptions: "Life insurance isn't about age, wealth, or dependents—it's about being prepared for the unexpected."

Real-Life Stories of Insufficient Coverage

I worked with the family of a young professional who thought their employer-provided policy was sufficient. When a tragic accident occurred, the family discovered that the group policy only covered one year of income, far less than what was needed to support their loved ones.

This family wasn't prepared even though they thought they had done everything right. It's a harsh reminder of why it's so important to evaluate your coverage and make sure it matches your goals.

Empowerment Through Understanding

Ultimately, life insurance is about empowerment. It's not just a product—it's a plan that protects the people, businesses, and values that matter most to you. By taking the time to understand your options, avoiding common pitfalls, and seeking expert guidance, you can ensure that your policy truly meets your goals.

Life insurance isn't a luxury or a one-size-fits-all solution. It's a highly personalized tool, and when designed properly, it can offer guarantees that provide lasting peace of mind. Let your policy work for you, not against you.

LIR can help you go from believing that your policy is the best option to knowing. We walk you through the explore, compare, and verify process with a fiduciary so you are empowered to decide what is right for you.

Now that you have a clearer understanding of how life insurance fits into your financial plan, let's explore the **LIR Life Insurance Types Triangle™**—a simple, visual tool designed to help you quickly grasp the three core types of life insurance commonly used in financial planning.

Life Insurance Types Triangle™

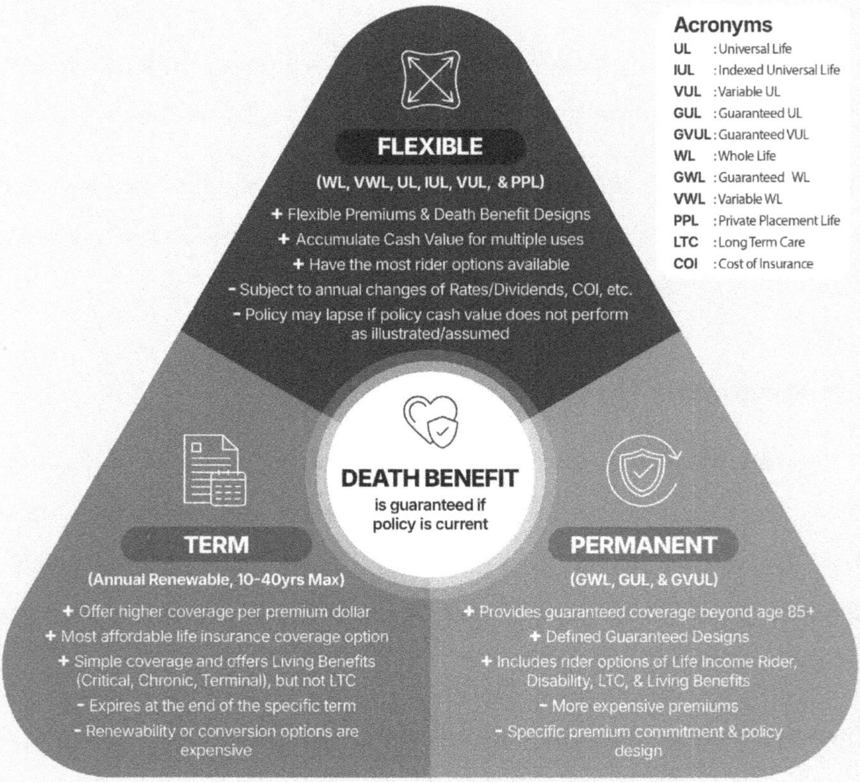

PLANNING QUESTIONS:

1) Limited Coverage/Protection for a specific term?
2) Build Cash Value for Retirement Supplement Income?
3) Estate Planning and/or Wealth Transfer Asset?

POLICY DESIGN QUESTIONS:

1) Policy Focus on Death Benefit, Cash Value Accumulation, or Both?
2) Increasing Death Benefit or Level Death Benefit?
3) Long Term Care Benefits Planning or Other Living Benefits (Critical, Chronic or Terminal Illness)?

CHAPTER FOUR

BUY, DON'T BE SOLD:

How the Industry Pushes Policies You Don't Need or are NOT the Best Value

Nobody likes to be sold, but everyone likes to buy.

– **Dr Earl Taylor,** trainer in leadership, sales, and interpersonal and communications skills

"Buy, don't be sold." A simple phrase, but in the world of life insurance, it's a game changer. Actively buying what is best for your needs is radically different from taking what the agent or broker has to sell. Plus, let's face it, very few of us like to be sold to.

I believe that you have to flip the script on the life insurance sales process to protect yourself. To empower you to do that, I am going to explain exactly how the process works and give you the tools to buy life insurance based on your specific needs and goals.

Too often, consumers approach life insurance as something they need to "get" because they've been told it's important, but they don't fully understand how to evaluate their options. Buying life insurance should be about empowerment, choosing a policy knowing it's the best value and will secure your future, not because someone convinced you to sign on the dotted line.

Unfortunately, the life insurance sales industry is structured to do the opposite. They know that it's not about offering the best products, but about being first to show what they think is best for you. Many agents and brokers are trained to sell, not serve, promoting what they've been taught and to promote only what's in their inventory rather than helping you find what truly meets your needs, as that is too complicated and will not pay them the most.

In this chapter, we'll explore the tactics used to sell life insurance, the systemic issues that perpetuate these practices, and how you can take back control of the process. We'll show you how to be an informed buyer, not just another sale.

Understanding the Sales-Driven Nature of Life Insurance

The life insurance industry isn't built around your needs, it's built around sales metrics. Life insurance sale professionals are often judged by how many policies they sell, how many appointments they book, and how many clients they convert. This sales-driven culture shapes every interaction, often at the expense of genuine guidance.

Let's break it down:

1. **Metrics Rule the Day**:
   They are evaluated on numbers. Did they meet their quota this month? If not direct quota, then it's their specific set sales goals

depending on their experience value. Did they push the "top" products? These metrics influence how they approach you, often making it less about your needs and more about their goals and keeping or advancing their sales career.

2. **Product-Focused Training**:
   They are trained to sell specific policies, not to provide comprehensive financial guidance. They may not know about or have access to the full range of options and specific financial planning strategies, meaning their recommendations are limited to what they know and are really just sales presentations.
3. **Pressure to Close**:
   The focus on closing sales creates a pressure-based environment for both the life insurance sales professional and the consumer. This pressure can lead to rushed decisions and policies that don't align with your financial goals and not exactly what you expected, which leads to the issues of buyer's remorse.

All this means that you may be sold on a policy that your agent or broker doesn't fully understand. If they don't understand it, but are selling it to meet their sales quota, what are the chances that it is the best option for you?

What "Buy, Don't Be Sold" Means in Practice

Buying life insurance is fundamentally different from being sold life insurance. When you buy, you are in control. You've done your research, evaluated your options, and made a decision based on what's best for you and your family.

When you're sold life insurance, the process looks very different:

- **The Agent or Broker Leads the Conversation**: Instead of empowering you to understand your options, they focus on guiding you towards particular products of their choosing.
- **Emotional Tactics Are Used**: Fear of the unknown or guilt about protecting your family is emphasized to push a quick decision.
- **Limited Options Are Presented**: You're only shown options that the life insurance sales professional knows of and can offer; and often they are the ones with high sales incentives.

"Buy, don't be sold" means flipping this script. It means:

- Own your time, ask questions, and demand clear, honest answers until you're fully satisfied.
- Explore and compare your options across multiple companies and platforms to learn and verify what is best
- Insisting on a fiduciary approach where your wants and needs always come first and there is no pressure to make any decisions.

Back to the Car Lot

Let's return once again to the analogy of buying a brand new car. Imagine walking onto a car lot with your heart set on a specific vehicle. You know you want a Porsche because it fits your needs perfectly: performance, reliability, and style. But somehow instead of visiting a Porsche dealership, you end up at a Land Rover dealership.

The salesperson knows they can't sell you a Porsche because they don't carry it. So, they focus on convincing you that a Land Rover is just as good, better, even! They'll highlight features you didn't ask for, gloss over the differences, and emphasize how lucky you are to be considering a Land Rover. Rather than tell you that the Porsche dealership is a mile down the road, they try to sell you on what they offer. Regardless of what you want or need.

This is how life insurance sales often work. Life insurance sales professionals sell what they have on their "lot." If they're captive, they can only offer policies from one company. Even independent brokers are often limited by representations with specific carriers and driven by the commission structures of certain products.

This isn't inherently malicious. Many agents and brokers genuinely believe in the products they're selling. However, that's not the same as helping you find what's truly best for your unique situation. At the end of the day, your needs and goals often aren't at the center of the process, unless you take control. Otherwise, their priorities will drive your decision-making for you.

The Sales Process in Life Insurance

Central to the "Buy, don't be sold to" mantra is understanding the motivations and training of the typical life insurance sales professionals. Generally, they operate in a sales-driven environment where metrics and incentives determine their advancement and success. In a pressure-based sales culture, advancement isn't measured by the quality of advice they provide or the satisfaction of their clients—it's judged simply by sales numbers.

Here are some metrics that drive life insurance sales professionals.

- **Prospecting Meetings:** How many potential clients did they meet?
- **Second Appointments Secured:** Did they convince the prospect to come back?
- **Policies Sold:** How many applications were submitted and premiums collected?
- **Referral Count:** How many referrals are they able to generate from their clients?

There is a pattern here. These metrics are centered on the salesperson and the company, not on you. They are often under immense pressure to hit these targets, and as a result, their focus shifts away from truly understanding your needs, let alone learning about other industry-leading products, financial planning, etc. Instead of acting as a counselor, they become a focused salesperson, intent on closing the deal rather than ensuring that what they are offering is best for you.

The Recruiting Process: Where It All Begins

The challenges in the life insurance sales process (and the root of the sales-centric culture) starts with how agents and independent agents who are associated with a marketing organization are recruited and trained. Many companies advertise life insurance sales as an opportunity to "be your own boss" or "earn unlimited income." These promises attract individuals with little to no experience in financial services, creating a revolving door of inexperienced agents and brokers.

Here's how the process typically unfolds:

1. **Recruiting**: All new agents are often brought in through flashy promises of high earnings and financial freedom. Many are drawn from network marketing recruitment organizations and others are through the traditional job postings.
2. **Limited Training**: Once brought on board, new recruits typically receive minimal training on the full range of life insurance products. Instead, their time is heavily focused on sales techniques and meeting production goals. Most are trained primarily on the company's own offerings, not the broader market options that might better suit a client's needs. Caught up in the promise of high income potential and the fast-paced sales environment, many agents prioritize prospecting and selling over truly understanding policy design and client suitability. In fact, many life insurance companies and marketing organizations expect them to sell at least 50 policies within their first year.
3. **Sell to Your Circle**: All new agents and brokers who are part of marketing organizations are greatly encouraged and even pressured to sell to friends and family, leveraging personal relationships to meet their initial training requirements and/or sales goals.

While this strategy might sound harmless or just good business, it can have serious consequences. Using trust built from personal relationships to push products creates a dynamic where the agent's and broker's goals are prioritized over the consumer's.

Selling to Family and Friends

So here is the dirty little insight—the sales-driven approach is designed to run through agents quickly. At first that may seem crazy, but think about it. Every new agent that comes in brings their list of contacts, fresh new people for the company to market to.

These new contacts are predisposed to trust the new agent. They deliver their friends and family on a silver platter to the company. When they have run through their contacts, the good (few) agents will have hit their metrics and continue with the company. The bad ones will move on, out of the industry or to another company promising them better income opportunities.

Insurance companies are fueled by actuaries. They know that they will run a high percentage of new agents through the process and they will not stay. They understand that the truth to getting a life insurance sale is often being the first to get to a prospect. So when the agent runs through their friends and family, they are often done with the company.

But what remains with the company? The friends and family that the agent signed up.

The life insurance sales process is not set up for your benefit. No matter what they tell you.

Consider this. Your good friend calls you and tells you that he is an accountant now. You let him do your taxes. After you submit the return and pay for the taxes, you find out that he was paid bonuses from the Feds for the taxes he could get you to pay. How would you feel?

Betrayed. And if you had known that, you would not have ever let him do your taxes.

This is how you need to think about your friend being your insurance agent. You need to understand the competing interests and you need a fiduciary to make sure yours are protected.

Most people know this drill. A friend starts selling life insurance and suddenly your phone is filled with messages from them. I will say one thing, life insurance sales training encourages tenacity. Now you know why.

If you have ever been on the receiving end of this tactic, you understand the drawbacks:

- **Pressure to Buy**: Personal relationships can make it difficult for prospects to say no, leading to purchases based on obligation rather than need.
- **Suboptimal Policies**: Friends and family may end up with policies that don't truly align with their goals, simply because the agent lacked the knowledge or independence to offer better options.
- **Strained Relationships**: When the focus is on sales rather than service, these interactions can damage personal relationships.

As a consumer, you have to ask yourself: Does this sound like the process you want to use to protect your family's future?

Why Trust Matters

Buying life insurance is one of the most important financial decisions you'll ever make. It's not just about protecting your income or paying off debts, it's about ensuring your loved ones have stability and security when they need it most.

Yet, the sales-driven nature of the industry often erodes trust. Consumers need to consider whether the policies they're being offered are truly in their best interest or simply the most profitable for the agent.

When you're sold life insurance rather than making an informed purchase, the consequences can be far-reaching and costly. One of the most immediate risks is overpaying for coverage. Many policies pushed by agents and brokers include unnecessary riders or overly complex features, driving up premiums without delivering real value. These added costs might not align with your actual needs, but they can certainly help boost the agent's and broker's commission.

Another common pitfall is receiving less coverage than you actually require. When an agent is focused on upselling additional features, the core purpose of the policy—adequate financial protection—can be overlooked. This leaves you vulnerable, with insufficient coverage to safeguard your family or achieve your long-term financial goals.

Even worse, the policies you're sold are often mismatched to your needs. Instead of designing a plan that aligns with your unique circumstances, agents frequently push products that are easier to sell or meet their sales quotas. The result? You could end up underinsured or locked into a policy that fails to meet your future objectives.

Finally, the reliance on personal relationships to drive sales can erode trust, not just in the individual agent, but in the entire life insurance industry. When friends or family members feel pressured to buy a policy, the transaction can sour otherwise strong relationships. This dynamic often leaves consumers feeling manipulated rather than supported, creating a lingering skepticism toward life insurance as a whole.

As long as the focus of the life insurance selling process is on the needs of the agent or the company that they represent, instead of your particular goals, you are being sold to. You are not "doing a solid" to make sure your buddy makes her quotas, you are risking your future goals.

Avoiding the Salesperson Trap

To protect yourself from being "sold" instead of truly guided, here are some steps you can take:

1. **Ask the Right Questions**:
    - Are you a captive agent and what companies can and can't you represent?
    - Do you belong to a marketing organization that provides you with incentives to recruit others to sell a certain amount of life insurance products to advance in the organization?
    - How are you compensated—through commission and/or other financial and marketing incentives?
    - What specific product planning experience and certifications do you have?
    - Do you also have an active securities license to talk about variable insurance products and investments?

- How long have you been a full time practicing agent or a broker?
- What specific life insurance products do you own yourself or do you have on your family?

2. **Do Your Research**:
   Every state has a Department of Insurance where you can check an agent's or broker's license status and background. For example, in California, you can search by name or license number directly on the Department of Insurance website. A quick Google search for "California life insurance license agent/broker check" will take you there.
3. **Get a Second Opinion**:
   Use unbiased resources like LifeInsuranceReview.com to understand your options, compare policies, and verify what they told you. Don't commit to a policy without reviewing it with an experienced fiduciary. There's a reason why the law provides for a 10-30 day free look period after you receive your policy, so consumers have time to thoroughly review their finished policy.
4. **Focus on Your Goals & Needs**:
   Keep the conversation centered on your specific wants and needs. If the agent or broker starts pushing products that don't align with your specific goals, or they don't offer clear answers, take a step back.

What Happens After You Are Sold (They Really Don't Want You to Know This)

Here's another uncomfortable truth: while many agents and brokers are well-meaning and genuinely want to help, the sales-driven structure of the industry means their financial incentive largely disappears once the policy is finalized. Their income is largely tied to making new sales, not to ongoing service or ensuring your policy continues to meet your needs over time. This is a major reason why most agents or brokers rarely offer proactive policy reviews, and why a large percentage leave the industry within just one to three years.

This reality raises a crucial question: how much of the process is truly about serving your best interests, and how much is about getting you to sign on the dotted line and waiting for the free look period to expire?

The Sales Process: A Carefully "Orchestrated Show"

Life insurance sales often resemble a well-rehearsed performance: what you see is carefully curated, while the real action happens behind the scenes. This "orchestrated show" misdirects consumers, focusing their attention on features and benefits that seem impressive but may not truly match their needs.

For example, an agent or broker might emphasize the cash value accumulation in a whole life or universal life policy, presenting it as a "savings" tool. What they might not explain is the uncertainty of the growth rate, the high fees that eat into returns, or the fact that withdrawing from the cash value reduces the death benefit. Similarly, they may highlight flexibility in premiums without fully disclosing the risks of insufficient funding over time.

The well-rehearsed presentation is reinforced by the agent's or broker's confidence, making it easy to trust their recommendations without digging deeper. But beneath the surface lies a system designed to prioritize sales over your best interest, steering you toward policies that benefit them or their company more than you.

Hidden Sales Incentives and the Commission-Driven Model

Most consumers don't realize the extent to which commission structures influence policy recommendations. Agents and brokers are paid a percentage of the first-year premium, which can range from 90% to over 100%, depending on the policy type. This may result in a conflict of interest:

- **Pushing Higher Premiums**: The larger the premium, the bigger their paycheck. This is one reason whole life policies are often recommended over term life—they come with significantly higher premiums and, therefore, higher commissions.
- **Favoring Complex Policies**: Policies with additional riders or investment components often carry higher commissions, incentivizing them to upsell features you might not need.
- **Company-Specific Rewards**: Many of them are further influenced by bonuses, contests, or luxury trips offered by their employer or affiliated insurers to hit sales targets.

These hidden incentives can lead to recommendations that don't meet your goals. Agents and brokers might push policies that generate higher payouts for them, even if simpler, more affordable options would better serve you.

The Problem with a "Close-First" Mentality

In an industry where sales are the only way to make money, agents and brokers are trained to focus on the close above all else. This creates a transactional dynamic, where the goal is to sell, and convert prospects into policyholders as quickly as possible. I like to call it the "Ready, Fire, Aim" approach.

While this approach might work in other industries, life insurance is fundamentally different. It's not just a product, it's a long-term financial commitment with significant implications for the future. Yet the sales process often prioritizes urgency over understanding, rushing you to make a decision without fully exploring your options.

When agents and brokers are too focused on the close, critical conversations are overlooked:

- Are the premiums sustainable for the long term?
- Does the policy include the coverage you actually need?
- How does this policy fit into your broader financial plan?

Without these discussions, you risk being sold a policy instead of buying a safeguard for your future.

Why Cash Value Life (Whole Life & Universal Life) Is Pushed Over Term Life

One of the clearest examples of commission-driven sales tactics is the preference for cash value life insurance over term life. Cash value life policies are often marketed as a "Swiss Army Knife" or "all-in-one" solution, combining life insurance with cash value accumulation. But for many consumers, term life provides a simpler and more cost-effective way to achieve their goals.

The Reality Behind Cash Value Life:

- **Higher Premiums**: Cash value life premiums can be five to ten times higher than term life for the same coverage amount.
- **Lower Immediate Value**: Most of your first-year premiums, and often up to the first ten years, are largely allocated to fees and commissions, resulting in minimal cash value growth.
- **Complexity**: Whole life policies include layers of features that are difficult for most consumers to fully understand, making it easier to be misled.

In contrast, term life is straightforward: you pay a low premium for a set amount of coverage over a specific period. For families on a budget or those with temporary financial obligations, term life often makes more sense.

So why are whole life and indexed universal life policies so heavily promoted? The answer lies in the commissions. Agents and brokers earn significantly more from cash value life policies than term, creating a strong financial incentive to steer clients in that direction, even when it's not the best fit.

Advice vs. Counsel: The Difference That Matters

When you work with a fiduciary or trusted advisor, the conversation shifts from sales to service. Instead of being sold a policy, you receive guidance that respects your goals and empowers you to make informed decisions.

Let's return to the earlier point about advice vs. counsel:

- **Advice**: A sales-focused agent or broker often dictates what you should buy, prioritizing products that benefit them most or that they are simply most familiar with. They typically avoid discussing or offering options outside their preferred scope.
- **Counsel**: A fiduciary listens to your needs, offers unbiased information and guidance, and empowers you to make informed decisions. They won't dictate what's best for you; instead, they'll help you clarify what you know is best for yourself.

At LIR, we believe in the power of counsel. Our process is designed to educate and empower you, ensuring that every decision you make is rooted in understanding and confidence. When you're respected, informed, and supported, you'll choose a policy that truly meets your needs—not one that serves someone else's agenda.

My estate planning attorney partner James often says, "The best policy is the one you choose for yourself."

This philosophy is manifested in LIR's core principles:

1. **Transparency**: We provide clear, unbiased information about your options, breaking down complex policies into terms you can understand.
2. **Empowerment**: By educating you about the pros and cons of different policies, we put the power back in your hands.
3. **Support**: We are a life insurance review company first, who is on the side of the consumer. Our only goal is to help you make decisions that align with your needs and goals.

Through our reviews, tools, and resources, we've helped countless individuals and families navigate the life insurance process with confidence.

Did Your Agent or Broker Discuss These Things With You?

When working with an agent or broker, ask yourself:

1. Did they explain clearly how they are compensated and clarify any potential conflict of interest?
2. Did they present multiple options with clear explanations, or just one or two?
3. Did they discuss how the policy fits into your specific financial plan?
4. Did they fully disclose the policy charges & fees and the policy internal rate of return report if it's a cash value policy?

5. Did they encourage you to take your time and get a second opinion, especially after they delivered the policy to you and explained about the 10-30 day free look period?

If the answer to any of these questions is "no," you may be at risk of being sold rather than empowered to buy what is best for you.

Don't Forget

Buying life insurance should never feel like a well-rehearsed show where what's presented is just too good to be true. You deserve transparency, respect, and the opportunity to make decisions based on your needs and time frame, not on someone else's incentives.

The sales-driven nature of the industry creates challenges, but with the right knowledge and guidance, you can navigate them confidently. Remember: the goal is not to find the most popular policy or the one with the most features, it's to find the policy that best fits you, your goals, and your budget.

The life insurance industry isn't inherently bad, it's the sales-driven culture that creates problems. When agents and brokers are judged by metrics like policies sold and the number of new referrals and appointments booked, their focus may shift away from you.

As you navigate the sales process, remember that buying life insurance is too important to leave to chance, so you should find a fiduciary life insurance expert who will only put you first. Take the time to ask questions, seek unbiased counsel, and ensure the policy you choose truly reflects your needs and goals. After all, you're not just buying a product—you're securing your future with a product that can protect it!.

CHAPTER FIVE

POLICY ILLUSTRATIONS

– The Danger of Assumptions and False Projections

If we choose, we can live in a world of comforting illusion.
– **Noam Chomsky,** Professor, the "father of American linguistics"

Projections and promises mean little if they don't hold up when you or your family needs them most.

When it comes to life insurance, the policy illustration is often the star of the sales process. These detailed projections are presented as if they hold the answers to every question you might have: How much will this policy cost? What benefits will it deliver? How will it perform over time? But as with most things in life, if it seems too good to be true, it probably is.

These policy illustrations can sometimes be more fairly categorized as "illusions."

Over the past two decades, I've reviewed countless life insurance policy illustrations. What consistently stands out is how easily these documents can mislead—even highly financially literate individuals, let alone agents and brokers with limited experience. The issue isn't just the dense language, the flood of numbers, or the fine print—it's the built-in assumptions that often paint an overly optimistic picture, crafted to promote and sell a specific product rather than to provide a clear, realistic understanding of how the policy may actually perform.

Policy illustrations often promise more than they can realistically deliver, and understanding where the dangers lie is critical. Remember the "Orchestrated Show" analogy? What do these illustrations conceal and what do they reveal?

Let's pull back the curtain on how illustrations work, what they really mean, and why it's vital to separate illusions from guarantees.

The Role of Policy Illustrations in Selling Life Insurance

Start with this key understanding: life insurance illustrations are primarily marketing tools. They're designed to show how a policy might perform over time, based largely on current assumptions, such as interest rates, dividend payouts, and market conditions. What many agents and brokers don't clearly explain is that these assumptions can change from year to year, sometimes significantly. Yet, illustrations are often used to paint an optimistic picture of the future, emphasizing projected growth in premiums, cash value, and death benefits, without adequately addressing the risks or variability behind those projections.

The intent of these illustrations is to give you, the buyer, confidence in your decision. They provide a framework to compare policies, evaluate costs, and understand potential outcomes. But here's the catch: these projections are not guaranteed.

For example, an Indexed Universal Life (IUL) illustration might show impressive cash value growth tied to the performance of a market index, such as the S&P 500 index. However, these projections are often based on overly optimistic assumptions about index returns and policy expenses. The fine print usually clarifies that the numbers are "non-guaranteed," but by then, the consumer may already be dazzled by the illusion of high returns possibilities. The same applies to whole life policies: dividend rates are not guaranteed and can fluctuate over time. Additionally, internal policy expenses often increase, which can reduce the net amount you receive when taking income/loans, often resulting in returns that fall short of what was originally illustrated.

When you understand the illustrations as an illusion, you can use critical thinking to make sure that you are not fooled by them. Imagine you went to a magic show and did not understand that it was an illusion. You might be genuinely convinced the levitation trick was real.

This chapter will help you understand policy illustrations so you can truly understand what you are being sold.

Decoding the Misleading Language in Illustrations

Why are policy illustrations marketing tools instead of guarantees? They are the misdirection part of the show. Policy illustrations are filled with industry jargon designed to make policies sound better than they really are. Terms like "projected values," "non-guaranteed elements," and "current assumptions" might seem straightforward, but they often mask the best-case scenario nature of the projections.

Let me break down a few examples of the misleading language commonly found in illustrations:

- **"Non-Guaranteed Elements"**
  This phrase refers to components of the policy, such as dividends or interest credits, that the insurance company is not obligated to provide. If the company's financial performance dips or if market conditions change due to lower interest rate environments, these elements could shrink or disappear altogether.
- **"Current Assumptions"**
  This term is shorthand for "if everything stays exactly as it is today." Interest rates remain high, market conditions remain favorable, and the insurer's expenses don't increase. Of course, we know the financial world doesn't work that way.
- **"Policy Projections"**
  Projections are hypothetical and based on a mix of guaranteed and non-guaranteed values. They are not promises and should not be treated as such.

It's easy to see how these terms can mislead you into believing you are getting a guaranteed outcome when, in reality, you're being shown a set of best-case scenarios. The disconnect occurs when these projections aren't clearly explained or are given more weight than they deserve.

Have you ever bought a shirt online without realizing it was from a less-than-reputable fashion brand? You see a shirt that you like and the price is right. You select the style, the size, and the color then place your order.

Then you receive a shirt that is the size you ordered but not the style or pattern from the ad. The quality and style do not match what you saw online. In fact, it looks nothing like what the model was wearing. Turns out that the model was the marketing department's best-case scenario for what you ordered, not the reality the shipping department sent you.

Life insurance should not be like this. You should not be sold what the model is wearing while unwittingly buying something else. To prevent this, you have to understand what is best-case scenario marketing and what is a guarantee.

Illustrations vs. Guarantees: Spotting the Difference

If you are sold solely on a policy illustration, you may not be buying what you think you are. Here is what you need to understand:

1. **Illustrations (The Illusions)**
   Illustrations often show the "best case" scenario—how a policy could perform under the maximum allowed assumed conditions by industry standards. These numbers are speculative, based on current rates, dividends, and market performance.

For example, an IUL might illustrate annual returns tied to a capped percentage of a market index. But the illustration won't prominently feature the fees, caps, or participation rates that limit actual returns. The illustration may further exclude the fact that the cap, participation rates, and even the specific index used to illustrate may change in the future as well, all at the discretion of the insurance company. As a result, the cash value may grow far slower than the numbers suggest.

2. **Guarantees (The Reality)**
   Guaranteed values are the elements of a policy the insurer is contractually obligated to provide, regardless of market conditions or internal company changes. These include:
   - Minimum interest rates on cash value.
   - Fixed premiums for term or whole life policies.
   - Guaranteed death benefits for the life of the policy if not lapsed.

Guarantees provide a safety net, ensuring that even if the market tanks or the insurer faces challenges, the basic benefits remain intact. But they also tend to be far less impressive than the non-guaranteed values shown in illustrations.

Many policies rely heavily on non-guaranteed elements to project impressive growth. This is where the danger lies: policyholders can be lulled into a false sense of security, assuming their policy will perform as illustrated without realizing the inherent risks involved.

Why This Matters

Policy illustrations aren't inherently bad, they're useful tools when understood correctly. The danger comes when they're presented as promises or when the buyer doesn't have the knowledge to separate fact from speculation.

As someone who's reviewed thousands of policies, I've seen the consequences of trusting illustrations without understanding their limitations. People base major financial decisions on these projections, often with no idea how much risk they're taking on.

Imagine planning your retirement around an IUL illustration that shows significant cash value growth. What happens if the policy underperforms? Suddenly, your retirement plans are in jeopardy, and you're scrambling to make up the difference.

This is why we emphasize the importance of understanding exactly what you are buying. At LIR we help consumers decode these illustrations, ensuring they understand what's guaranteed and what's speculative.

The Danger of Optimistic Projections

There is a reason that life insurance agents and brokers use projections, they help close deals. While life insurance policy illustrations are powerful tools, their power cuts both ways. When used responsibly, they can help you understand how your policy is designed to work. But too often, they are misutilized by sales-driven agents and brokers to paint a rosy, overly optimistic picture of what a policy might deliver.

These illustrations rely on assumptions about the future—assumptions that are, at best, uncertain and, at worst, misleading. When market conditions change or internal expenses rise (and they will!), the actual performance of a policy can fall short of what was promised. This gap between expectation and reality can leave consumers feeling betrayed, locked into policies that no longer serve their needs, or worse, facing financial hardship.

Questions to Separate Fact from Hype

One of the most effective ways to avoid being misled by policy illustrations is to ask the right questions. My partner James shares, "The key to understanding a policy isn't in the numbers—it's in the assumptions behind them."

Here are some critical questions to ask when reviewing an illustration:

1. **What Assumptions Are These Projections Based On?**
   - What are the interest rates, market returns, or dividend rates used in this illustration?
   - Are these numbers guaranteed, or are they subject to change every year?
   - Can the floor, caps, and the illustration rates be changed, if so, what are the parameters?
2. **What Are the Policy's Guaranteed Values?**
   - What is the minimum cash value growth or interest rate?
   - How does the guaranteed death benefit compare to the projected one?
3. **What Are the Policy Costs?**
   - What fees, charges, or expenses are deducted from the cash value?
   - How do these costs impact the policy's long-term performance?
4. **What Happens If Assumptions Change?**
   - If interest rates drop or expenses rise, how will this affect the policy?

    - Is there a risk of the policy lapsing if performance doesn't meet expectations?
    - What stress testing of the returns can be shown?
    - How do the assumed/projected rates affect the internal rates of return (IRR) on the policy cash value and death benefit?
5. **What Is the Agent's or Broker's Incentive?**
    - Are certain products being promoted due to higher commissions or any financial incentives?

By asking these questions, you can cut through the hype and get to the heart of what the policy truly offers.

The Difference Between Being Sold and Having Someone on Your Side

When you're being sold a policy, the focus is on closing the deal. The agent or broker may highlight the benefits while glossing over the risks, leaving you to make a decision based on incomplete information.

Remember, you should be able to explore, compare, and verify clearly. This can be difficult when all the policy illustrations are based on different assumptions and guarantees. You need to be able to compare apples to apples, not apples to an idea of a perfect fruit.

This is why when you have someone on your side that is an advocate, like a fiduciary advisor or an independent reviewer, the conversation changes. The goal is no longer to sell but to empower you with the knowledge and tools you need to make the right choice.

At LIR, we prioritize education and transparency. We take the time to explain the fine print, identify potential red flags, and ensure you fully understand what you're committing to. This approach not only helps you avoid costly mistakes but also gives you confidence that your policy truly lines up with your goals.

Breaking Down the Language of Policy Illustrations

One of the most frustrating aspects of life insurance illustrations is the complex, jargon-filled language they use. For example, you might see something like this:

"Projected cash value is based on current assumptions, including a 6.5% annual crediting rate that is non-guaranteed."

Take a minute to decipher what you think this means. On the surface, this might seem straightforward. But here's what it really means:

- **Projected Cash Value**: This is hypothetical and may not reflect the actual performance of the policy.
- **Current Assumptions**: These are subject to change. If interest rates drop or dividends are reduced, the cash value will grow more slowly, or not at all.
- **Non-Guaranteed Rates**: The insurance company is not obligated to pay a specific dividend rate for Whole Life policies, or it can guaranteed a specific credit interest rate each year for Universal Life type policies.

Without someone to help you interpret this language, it's easy to misinterpret the illustration as a promise rather than a possibility. This is why a second opinion is so important. An independent reviewer can help you understand the true meaning behind the numbers and ensure you're not being misled.

The Importance of a Second Opinion

Life insurance is a long-term commitment, and making the wrong choice can have lasting and compounding consequences. That's why we always recommend getting a second opinion before purchasing a policy.

A second opinion can help you:

- Identify discrepancies between projected and guaranteed values.
- Understand the impact of fees and charges on policy performance.
- Compare the policy to other options that might better align with your goals.

At LIR, we've built our process around this principle. Our independent reviews give you the clarity and confidence you need to make informed decisions, free from the pressure of a sales-driven environment.

Keep in Mind

While optimistic policy illustrations may appear appealing, they are no substitute for careful analysis and informed decision-making. Understanding the assumptions behind the numbers, asking critical questions, and seeking an independent review are essential steps to avoid being misled.

Life insurance is far too important to approach casually. With the right guidance, you can cut through the confusion, make well-informed choices, and secure a policy that truly aligns with your goals, not just one that looks good on paper.

At the end of the day, projections are not promises. And illusions provide no certainty for your loved ones.

CHAPTER SIX

CONFLICTS OF INTEREST AND IGNORANCE

– What They Don't Want You to Know

Dear Policyholder,

I am your life insurance policy. Though I remain quietly in the background, my purpose is deeply aligned with yours—to provide for your needs and for the ones you love, especially when you no longer can.

Today, it is your responsibility to provide for your family and loved ones. As you fulfill that important role, I stand ready—made possible by your foresight and commitment—and prepared for the day when I must step forward and carry that responsibility in your place.

Because of your careful diligence—your research, thoughtful questions, and thorough verification—you can be confident that I am the right policy for your needs. You did not rush. You did not guess. You made an informed, intentional decision. And because of that, you can move forward with peace of mind, knowing your family is protected by a plan that truly fits.

There may be moments when the cost of maintaining me feels like just another obligation. But remember: I am not just a policy—I am a promise. One day, when your journey ends, mine will begin—supporting your loved ones with the care, stability, and protection you planned for all along. And if life brings unexpected hardship while you are still here, I may even be able to step in early—because that, too, is part of the promise.

You've done your part with care and intention, so there is no need for doubt. You chose wisely—and I will be here, ready when the time comes.

With enduring purpose,
Your Life Insurance Policy

-LIR's version of "Dear Policyholder" letter

When you sit down with a life insurance agent or broker, you expect to receive expert guidance tailored to your unique situation. After all, buying life insurance is one of the most important financial decisions you'll make. It's about protecting your family, securing your future, and achieving peace of mind. But here's the harsh truth: the life insurance sales industry is not designed with your best interests at heart.

The letter above is LIR's critical take on the classic "Dear Policyholder" letter, originally crafted to appeal to emotions rather than promote careful review. Too often, it distracts from the importance of thoroughly evaluating the final delivered policy. The underlying message: having a policy is enough, no need to explore options, understand the details, or reassess if it still fits your needs. Just sign, pay premiums, and skip a second opinion.

This is how the relationship works between you and life insurance sales professionals. It's structured around a series of conflicts of interest and incentives that often lead to decisions that benefit agents, brokers, and their affiliated companies, more than consumers. And what's even more troubling? Many agents and brokers don't even realize the limitations of the advice they're providing. This "conflict of ignorance" isn't always intentional, but it can be just as damaging.

You may wonder how I know this. Personal experience. I once was the young agent who believed everything my company was telling me. I believed that I was offering families the absolute best protection on the market. And I was even told that I'm an independent broker, able to represent all life insurance companies and do what's best for my clients.

I wasn't.

For the first five years of my career, I didn't know nearly as much as people assumed I did. I lacked the technical knowledge, real-world planning experience, and the freedom to work with companies offering the most competitive options. At the time, the life insurance industry was far less transparent and less regulated, making it difficult to access clear, unbiased information, even as a licensed financial advisor.

Everything changed in February 2011, when I helped process the death benefit for a client who had passed away. I had sold him the policy in 2008, and at the time, I genuinely believed it was the best choice available. That belief came from what I had been told and trained to believe. But standing with his family, I realized they could have been in a much stronger financial position if I had known then what I would come to learn just a few years later. There were better-value policies available, including some that could have delivered at least 30 percent more in death benefit. I wasn't aware of them. I had trusted the people who recruited me into the industry, assuming they had all the answers. But they didn't, and I didn't yet have the knowledge or confidence to question what I had been taught.

That experience left me with a deep sense of regret. I knew I could have done more if I had known more. It also became a defining moment in both my personal and professional journey. I decided that I would never again let limited training or a firm's restricted offerings keep me from doing what is truly in the best interest of the people I serve.

That moment ultimately inspired me to launch my own agency, Life Insurance Review (LIR) Insurance Solutions, founded on a clear mission to always put the client first.

Since then, I have committed to continually growing my knowledge, improving the tools and resources available to my clients, and staying in the best position to serve those who trust me with their financial future. I built this firm on the belief that we should never settle. We must always aim higher, think deeper, and provide the most thoughtful, effective solutions for every individual and family we serve.

In this chapter, we'll explore how these conflicts arise, why they persist, and what you can do to protect yourself from being misled or underserved.

The Conflict of Interest—How the System Is Stacked Against You

The life insurance industry is built on sales, not service. Agents and brokers are compensated primarily through commissions, which are based on the premiums of the policies they sell. The bigger the policy, the bigger the paycheck. This creates a glaring conflict of interest: the financial incentives for agents or brokers and companies are often at odds with what's best for you.

How Commissions Shape Recommendations

Imagine you're deciding between a term life policy and a whole life policy. The term policy is affordable, straightforward, and meets your needs, while the whole life policy includes features you don't really want, like cash value accumulation, but comes with a much higher premium.

In an ideal world, your life insurance sales professional would recommend the term policy because it is in line perfectly with your goals. But in reality, agents and brokers earn far more from whole life policies because the premiums are significantly higher. This incentive can subtly (or not so subtly) shape the advice you receive. An agent or broker might emphasize the "investment" aspect of a whole life policy, downplaying its higher cost or its limitations compared to term coverage.

Consider a scenario where an agent or broker presents a whole life policy as a "smart investment" for retirement. They may highlight the potential cash value growth but avoid discussing the higher premiums you'll pay or the fact that term coverage would provide the same death benefit for a fraction of the cost. This selective presentation is driven by the structure of commissions, which reward agents more generously for selling whole life policies.

Sales Goals and Incentives

Beyond commissions, agents and brokers are often under pressure to meet strict sales goals (they no longer refer to them as "quotas") and productivity requirements of prospecting for new recruits to join their sales team and/or potential customers. These incentives can take many forms:

- **Promotional or End-of-Quarter Pushes**: Agents and brokers may call you out of the blue with an urgent pitch for a "great new plan or idea" that's supposedly perfect for you. In reality, they're likely trying to hit a sales target.
- **Luxury Rewards**: Some companies offer incentives like paid luxury conferences, jewelry gifts, sports car leases, and recognition at company events for top-performing agents and brokers.

- **Product-Specific Bonuses**: Certain policies or features may come with additional rewards for the agent or broker, steering them toward upselling or promoting specific products.

The influence of these incentives cannot be overstated. An agent or broker working to qualify for a bonus trip to the Bahamas may prioritize selling policies that help them achieve that goal, even if those policies aren't the best fit for their clients. This creates a conflict where the agent's or broker's financial motivations overshadow their responsibility to provide unbiased advice.

The Influence of Captive Relationships

Another layer of conflict comes from captive agents, who work exclusively for one insurance company, or even independent agents who work with a big financial company. They are trained to sell only that company's products or their preferred product partners, regardless of whether those products are the best fit for you. If you're working with a captive agent or an independent agent who works with a big financial company, your choices will be limited to what's "on the menu" at their company, even if better options exist elsewhere.

For instance, if a captive agent's company specializes in term policies but you need a whole life policy, you'll likely be steered toward a product that doesn't meet your goals. The result? You're paying more for features you don't need while missing out on better, more bespoke alternatives.

The limitations of captive agents or even independent agents working with a big financial company extend beyond the policies they sell. Their training often focuses exclusively on their company's products and their preferred list of partner products, leaving them with a narrow understanding of the broader insurance market. This lack of perspective can lead to recommendations that are not only self-serving but also poorly informed.

Brokers Aren't Always the Solution

At first glance, brokers might seem like a better option because they can sell policies from multiple insurers. However, even brokers are often limited by the relationships they have with specific companies. They may prioritize policies that offer higher commissions or bonuses, further narrowing your options. Whether you're working with a captive agent or a broker, the industry and system are stacked against you.

Imagine if you are an agent or broker and you are constantly pushing certain products, with various company representatives telling you why their products are the best and why you should be selling them to all your clients. How would this make you feel?

A broker might present themselves as an independent advisor, but if they're contracted with only a handful of insurers, their independence is limited and biased. Not to mention they may have limited financial planning experience and/or knowledge. All these important factors must be taken into account when choosing who you're working with. Unfortunately there can be this false sense of security for consumers, who believe they're exploring a wide range of options when, in reality, they're seeing only a curated selection that benefits the broker.

Why Transparency Matters

The lack of transparency in the life insurance sales industry exacerbates these conflicts. Most consumers have no idea how much their agent or broker is earning in commissions or how those commissions and added-on financial incentives influence the recommendations they receive. This opacity allows conflicts of interest to flourish, leaving consumers vulnerable to being misled.

Transparency is not just about disclosing commissions; it's about providing consumers with the information they need to make informed decisions. This includes clear explanations of policy features, unbiased assessments of their pros and cons, and the presentation of multiple options to ensure the best fit for the client's needs.

The Conflict of Ignorance—When Agents or Brokers Don't Know Any Better

One of the most unsettling aspects of the life insurance industry is how little many agents and brokers know about the products they're selling. This is the "conflict of ignorance," and it stems from how agents and brokers are recruited, trained, and incentivized to operate. One important observation is that most agents and brokers spend the majority of their time prospecting, selling, and receiving training on how to improve sales—rather than deepening their knowledge of life insurance products or engaging in comprehensive financial planning.

Limited Training and Narrow Perspectives

The barrier to entry for becoming a life insurance agent or broker is remarkably low. Many newcomers enter the field with little to no financial background or insurance expertise. Training is typically centered on how to sell the specific products they're authorized to offer, rather than gaining a comprehensive understanding of the broader range of life insurance solutions, or learning how to evaluate which options truly serve the client's best interests.

For example, a captive agent or independent agent who's part of a marketing organization might spend their training period memorizing the selling points of certain flagship cash value life policies without gaining any understanding of how term or comparable life policies from competitors could serve clients better. This limited perspective leaves agents and brokers ill-equipped to provide clients with comprehensive, unbiased guidance.

To make matters worse, many agents are encouraged to sell to their personal networks—family and friends. This approach leverages trust and familiarity but often results in inappropriate policy recommendations. A well-meaning but undertrained agent may sell their uncle a costly whole life policy simply because it's the only product they're familiar with.

For instance, an agent or broker might showcase a whole life policy's projected cash value at retirement age, emphasizing how it could supplement income. However, these projections often rely on best-case scenarios, assuming consistent interest rates or investment returns that may not reflect market realities. The fine print and internal rate of return

(IRR) report may reveal that the actual cash value could be much lower—but only if the client knows to look for it.

Agents and brokers may also downplay the impact of fees or penalties associated with accessing the policy's cash value, creating the impression that these funds are more accessible and beneficial than they truly are. Without clear explanations, consumers are left to interpret complex charts and figures on their own, often making decisions based on incomplete or misleading information.

The Impact of Incentives on Ignorance

While some agents and brokers knowingly misdirect clients, many are simply unaware of the limitations of their own advice. This "conflict of ignorance" is perpetuated by the industry's incentive structures. Agents and brokers are often incentivized to sell specific types of policies or products that further the company goals rather than client needs. As a result, even well-meaning agents and brokers can unknowingly push clients toward suboptimal solutions.

For example, an agent or broker might recommend a universal life policy with an indexed growth component because it's presented as a "versatile" option. However, the agent or broker may not fully understand how the indexing mechanism works or the potential downsides, such as caps on growth or the impact of increasing fees. The client, relying on the agent's or broker's expertise, is left with a policy that doesn't match with their specific long-term financial goals.

Marketing vs. Reality

Life insurance companies invest heavily in marketing to make their products appear attractive and trustworthy. Glossy professional brochures and polished illustration templates can create the illusion of a perfect policy, but they rarely tell the whole story. For instance, a policy may be advertised as offering "flexible premiums," but the fine print might reveal that skipping a premium could deplete the policy's cash value and lead to eventual lapse.

Similarly, some policies are marketed as having "living benefits," such as the ability to withdraw funds in case of critical illness. While these features can be valuable, they often come with restrictions or higher cost of the death benefit reduction that aren't immediately apparent. Agents and brokers may highlight these benefits to close a sale without fully explaining their limitations, leaving clients with unrealistic expectations.

How Ignorance Harms Consumers

The consequences of this ignorance are far-reaching. Clients may end up:

- **Overpaying for Coverage**: Purchasing expensive whole life or universal life policies when a term policy would have sufficed.
- **Underinsured**: Accepting a policy with insufficient death benefits, often due to higher costs compared to other options, or because of misaligned priorities.
- **Locked into Inflexible Policies**: Committing to long-term contracts that don't adapt to changing financial circumstances; or policies that may have rising costs and internal expenses.

- **Poor Policy Cash Value Performance:** Consumers may find that after years of consistently funding their policy, the performance failed to come close to what was originally illustrated by the agent or broker. This can have catastrophic consequences in cases where a consumer invested in a poor-performing policy, and now they are older and no longer qualify with an ideal health rating.

The Need for Independent Oversight

Navigating these challenges requires more than just diligence on your part, however recognizing what is happening will give you the power of knowledge. Independent oversight and fiduciary guidance are essential to ensure that clients receive unbiased, informed advice. At LIR, we specialize in cutting through the noise to help consumers make decisions based on facts, not sales pitches.

Empowering Consumers—Navigating the Industry with Confidence

While the challenges of conflicts of interest and ignorance in the life insurance sales industry are daunting, consumers don't have to navigate them alone. Empowerment begins with education, awareness, and the guidance of independent experts who prioritize your needs over their commissions.

Advice vs. Counsel

One of the key distinctions in the life insurance industry is the difference between advice and counsel. Advice is often shaped by sales incentives, hitting sales goals, and limited training. It's what an agent and broker tells you based on their own priorities. Counsel, on the other hand, focuses on your unique goals and empowers you to make informed decisions yourself.

At LIR, we provide counsel, not advice. We are consumer advocates. Our mission is to equip consumers with the knowledge and tools they need to evaluate policies objectively. This approach ensures that you're not being sold to but are instead empowered to buy what truly meets your needs.

Important Questions

To make informed decisions, it's essential to ask the right questions. I realize that these are not easy to ask, but the answers will shed light on areas that will help you make an informed decision. Here are some examples:

- **What are the agent's or broker's commissions?** Transparency about compensation can reveal potential conflicts of interest.
- **What other options are available?** If you're presented with only one or two policies, it's worth questioning if better options exist.
- **What are the limitations and risks?** Understanding the potential downsides of a policy ensures you're not caught off guard later.

Avoiding the Orchestrated Show

As I have said, the life insurance sales process is often a well-rehearsed show, with agents and brokers directing your attention to certain features while distracting you from potential downsides. For example, an agent might emphasize a policy's cash value growth while glossing over its high fees, or they may avoid explaining other, potentially better, options. Recognizing these tactics can help you stay focused on what truly matters: finding a policy that aligns with your goals.

How LifeInsuranceReview.com (LIR) Can Help

At LIR, we take a different approach. Our goal is to provide unbiased, comprehensive reviews that empower consumers to make informed decisions. Here's how we do it:

- **Comprehensive Policy Analysis**: We break down complex policies into clear, understandable terms, highlighting both the benefits and potential drawbacks.
- **Objective Comparisons**: Unlike agents and brokers who are tied to specific companies, we provide side-by-side comparisons of multiple policies from various insurers.
- **Fiduciary Commitment**: As fiduciaries, we are legally obligated to act in your best interest, ensuring that our recommendations align with your needs and goals.

A Better Way Forward - Knowledge, Not Ignorance

The life insurance sales industry's structure, built on conflicts of interest and pervasive ignorance, is stacked against you. Agents, whether captive or not, are incentivized by commissions, hitting sales goals, and many financial incentives that often undermine the quality of the advice they provide. Their loyalty is rarely to you or your best interests. This isn't always a case of deliberate harm—many agents and brokers simply lack the training or perspective to understand how their recommendations fall short of what their clients truly need and can benefit from the most.

This is why taking control of your life insurance decisions is so critical. By recognizing the potential conflicts of interest and the limitations of the agent or broker's expertise, you can begin to protect yourself from being misled. Transparency, education, and independent advice are the keys to making informed choices that serve your best interests, not someone else's bottom line.

At LIR, we believe that the consumer deserves better than just getting life insurance coverage; our priority is to make sure each person gets the best coverage for themselves and not be sold to. We offer fiduciary-first guidance designed to empower you. We cut through the noise, exposing the gaps in knowledge and conflicts in motivation that plague the industry. We want you to be equipped with the tools and knowledge you need to choose a policy that aligns with your goals and priorities, not someone else's agenda.

Ultimately, the power lies with you. By asking the right questions, seeking unbiased reviews, and staying vigilant against marketing misdirection, you can take charge of your financial future. Don't settle for ignorance, insist on being informed.

Metrics Matter

One of the most overlooked aspects of life insurance is how agents and brokers can manipulate metrics to make policies appear more attractive. For example, an illustration might show favorable outcomes for a hypothetical client: a 45-year-old nonsmoker in excellent health, without disclosing that the same policy could be significantly less beneficial for someone with a different profile. Understanding these nuances is critical to making informed decisions.

Taking Control of Your Financial Future

Ultimately, the key to navigating the life insurance industry is taking control of the decision-making process. This means:

1. **Educating Yourself**: Learn about the different types of policies and their features.
2. **Asking Tough Questions**: Challenge agents and brokers to provide clear, honest answers about commissions
3. **Partnering With A Third-Party Advisor:** A fiduciary like LIR can help you evaluate your options and make the best decision for you, free of conflicts.

Here's LIR's Top 8 Do's & Don'ts of Buying Life Insurance:

DON'T BE SOLD

THE TOP 8 DO'S & DON'TS OF BUYING LIFE INSURANCE

Top DO'S

1. **EDUCATE YOURSELF on the basics** of life insurance including the different types.
2. **CLEARLY DEFINE your needs and goals** before speaking to an agent/broker/advisor.
3. **DOCUMENT all communications** and copies of all relevant documents.
4. **TAKE YOUR TIME** and never feel pressured to make any immediate decision.
5. **INSIST on seeing multiple options and quotes/illustrations** from different reputable insurance companies.
6. **VERIFY the agent/broker/advisor limitations** of products and specific company offering due to their company structure and/or licenses.
7. **DEMAND TRANSPARENCY** of agent/broker/advisor on their compensation and potential conflicts.
8. **USE THE "FREE LOOK PERIOD"** to review the final policy and get a second independent opinion.

Top DON'TS

1. **BUYING a policy you don't fully understand.**
2. **BUYING a policy just because of a personal connection or referral.**
3. **ASSUMING Cash Value Policies are guaranteed to perform as told/sold.**
4. **ASSUMING Permanent Life Insurance is truly "permanent" and can never lapse.**
5. **RELY SOLEY on the Policy Illustration(s)/Quote(s) to make your purchasing decision.**
6. **OVERLOOKING OR NOT understanding the Annual Policy Charges & Fees Disclosure Page.**
7. **OVERLOOKING OR NOT understanding the Policy Internal Rate of Return (IRR) Report.**
8. **SURRENDER/REPLACE an existing policy without a thorough and objective comparison of cost & benefits.**

CHAPTER SEVEN

THE FREE LOOK PERIOD

– Your Last Line of Defense

Trust but verify.

– **Russian Proverb,** often quoted by President Ronald Reagan

We have spent plenty of time discussing how the deck can be stacked against you in the life insurance buying process. How can you trust what your broker or agent tells you? Finally, we reach a point where you regain your power. Even if you succumbed to pressure-based sales and promising policy illustrations, and already signed on the dotted line, you still have one last line of defense. The free look period.

I have told you how important it is to explore, compare, and verify. Now is the time to put that into action.

The most powerful tool in your arsenal as a consumer is the free look period, a mandatory provision in every life insurance policy. It is your right, even if no one mentions it to you.

Think of it as your last line of defense against agents, brokers, or insurers who may have prioritized their own interests over yours. This chapter explores the free look period, what it is, why it's so important, and how it can protect you from a decision you might regret.

What Is the Free Look Period?

The free look period is a window of time, typically lasting between 10 to 30 days depending on the state where the policy is issued, during which you can review your new life insurance policy after purchase. If you decide the policy isn't a good fit for your goals, you can cancel it for a full refund, no questions asked. It's essentially a "cooling-off" period that gives you the freedom to explore, compare, and verify your decision without a financial penalty.

This period is legally mandated in all U.S. states so that consumers have an opportunity to scrutinize the details of their policy outside the pressure-based sales environment. It's a chance to verify that the policy you are buying meets your goals and needs—not just what the agent sold you on.

Why Was the Free Look Period Enacted?

The free look period didn't exist in the early days of the life insurance industry. Back then, policies were often sold through aggressive sales tactics, with little to no transparency about the terms or conditions. Consumers were pressured into purchasing policies they didn't fully understand, only to discover later that the coverage didn't meet their expectations or needs.

Recognizing the imbalance of power between consumers and insurance companies, state regulators introduced the free look period as a safeguard. Its purpose is simple but critical: to protect consumers from being locked into contracts they don't fully understand.

This consumer-friendly provision was enacted to address several key issues:

- **Pressure-Based Sales Tactics:** Agents often rely on the emotional intensity of their pitch to close a sale. The free look period removes the immediate pressure, giving you the space to think clearly about your decision.
- **Complex Policy Language:** Insurance contracts are notoriously difficult to understand, often filled with jargon and fine print. The free look period allows you time to consult with a trusted advisor or expert to ensure you comprehend what you're signing up for. In many cases, the initial illustration is different from the final illustration at policy issue
- **Coverage Clarity:** Many consumers discover after purchase that their policy includes features they don't need or excludes ones they do. The free look period provides a critical opportunity to identify and rectify these ambiguities.

Why the Free Look Period Is So Important

If there's one takeaway from this book, it's this: the free look period is the greatest tool you have to make sure you are not sold something that is not a fit for you. Your agent or broker may not tell you about the free look period or may just brush over its importance, even though they're required by law to provide an adequate explanation. Why is it often avoided or ignored? Because it disrupts the sales process and more importantly encourages the consumer to get a second opinion to review what they were sold. Life Insurance sale professionals rely on your initial commitment and enthusiasm to make the sale. They know that given more time to think, some consumers will decide against the policy they've been sold. Plus, in the typical sales process, life insurance professionals need to move on to the next sale to meet their set sales goals for advancements.

So now that you know about the free look period, what should you focus on? The free look period isn't just a cancellation window—it's your opportunity to strip away the sales pitch and examine the policy with clear, informed eyes. This is your time to ask yourself the right questions:

- Do I fully understand what this policy offers—and how it compares to other strong options available in the market?
- Does this policy truly align with my financial goals—or could there be a better fit that offers more flexibility, growth potential, or protection?
- Are there any exclusions, fees, or limitations that weren't clearly explained to me upfront?
- Do I understand how the policy was designed, including the assumptions in the illustration and how it fits into my overall financial strategy?
- Have I done my due diligence on the agent or broker—including their experience, credentials, and whether they're affiliated with a company or marketing organization that influences their recommendations?

- Is there anything unclear that I need to verify before fully committing?

The free look period gives you a powerful tool, a measuring stick to evaluate whether this policy truly stands out among others. Use this time wisely to confirm that what you've been sold is in your best interest and not just in someone else's sales plan.

What You Stand to Lose

Canceling a life insurance policy after the free look period can result in financial penalties or losses depending on the type of policy you have and how long you've held it. Here's a quick overview of potential financial consequences:

1. Loss of Premium Payments (Term Life Insurance)

If you cancel a term life insurance policy after the free look period, you typically won't receive any refunds for the premiums you've already paid. Since term life insurance doesn't build cash value, there's no financial return for early cancellation. Essentially, the premiums paid up to that point are lost.

2. Surrender Charges (Permanent Life Insurance)

For whole life, universal life, or variable life insurance policies, which include a cash value component, canceling the policy often incurs surrender charges. These charges are fees levied by the insurer to offset the costs of issuing the policy and managing it over time.

- **Surrender periods** typically last 10 years, depending on the policy, with charges being higher in the earlier years and gradually decreasing over time.
- **Surrender charges** can be substantial, reducing the cash value payout significantly. For example if your policy has a cash value of $20,000 in the fourth year and you choose to surrender it, you could lose half or more of that cash value balance, upon policy cancellation.

3. Loss of Cash Value Growth

When you cancel a policy with a cash value component, you forfeit any future potential growth. Policies like whole life or indexed universal life may have projected cash value increases that would have been realized over time. By canceling, you stop the compounding growth of these funds.

4. Tax Implications

Canceling a policy can result in taxable income under certain conditions:

- If your policy has accrued a cash value greater than the total premiums paid, the difference is considered taxable income, if the policy is canceled.
- For example, if you've paid $10,000 in premiums but the cash surrender value is $12,000, the $2,000 gain may be subject to ordinary income tax, upon policy cancellation.

5. Loss of Insurance Coverage

Once you cancel a life insurance policy, you lose the protection it provides. If you decide to purchase a new policy later, you may face:

- **Higher premiums** due to increased age or health changes.
- **Limited coverage options** if your health has declined since purchasing the original policy.
- **Waiting periods** for certain benefits if the new policy includes clauses like contestability or suicide exclusions.

While the free look period offers a penalty-free opportunity to reassess your decision, canceling a life insurance policy after that period can lead to financial penalties, tax liabilities, and a loss of valuable coverage.

Your Way Out of Pressure-Based or Misleading Sales

Buying life insurance can be exhausting. You're subjected to presentations, pitches, and a level of emotional persuasion that can make anyone doubt their choices. During the sales process, it's easy to focus solely on what the life insurance sales professional highlights: the promised benefits, the appealing projections, or the compelling emotional stories. However, the details that matter most to you are often omitted.

This is where the free look period comes in. It's your opportunity to escape the pressure and objectively review your decision. With no sales scripts or persuasive tactics, you have the peace and time to examine your policy and confirm if it truly meets your needs.

What the Policy Says vs. What You Were Told

One of the most significant advantages of the free look period is that it gives you the opportunity to read the actual policy language. What's on paper might not align with what you were sold. For example:

- **Riders and Features:** Were you told that certain riders, like a disability waiver or accelerated death benefits, were included? The policy might say otherwise.
- **Premium Adjustments:** Did the agent or broker downplay the possibility of premium increases or fees? The fine print might reveal a different story.
- **Cash Value Projections:** Are the cash value growth rates overly optimistic? What set of data was chosen to show the favorable results? Take this time to verify whether those numbers are guaranteed or hypothetical.

The free look period allows you to separate facts from sales hype so that you're fully informed before committing to a policy that might not be what you were sold on.

The Free Look Period as Empowerment

The free look period isn't just about avoiding mistakes—it's about empowerment. It levels the playing field, giving you time to understand your policy and make changes if necessary. During this period, you can:

1. **Explore:** Get an unbiased review of the policy and what it means for your financial future.
2. **Compare:** Use the time to research other competative policies and determine whether your current choice is truly the best fit.
3. **Verify:** Contact your agent or broker for clarification on any terms or features that seem unclear.

At LIR, we are committed to empowering you to get the policy that best meets your needs and financial goals. We believe that the free look period is the greatest tool in your arsenal to make sure that you are getting exactly what you need.

The Payment Paradox: Why the Free Look Period Is Critical

In most cases, insurers require you to make a payment or provide binding authorization before they issue your policy documents. This creates a paradox: you're asked to commit financially before fully understanding the details of your policy. Life insurance sales professionals may summarize the highlights, but until you receive the actual contract, you won't see the fine print that determines your rights, coverage, and obligations.

This is where the free look period becomes invaluable. It provides a post-purchase opportunity to evaluate the full terms of your policy without the pressure of the sales process. During this window, you can cancel the policy without penalties, which is the truth to protecting your best interests.

The key here is that this period removes the pressure of an immediate sale. While your agent might focus on selling the benefits and simplifying the complex, the free look period allows you to revisit the (often complicated) details and verify whether the policy meets your financial goals. Without this window, you could be locked into a policy that's difficult to change or cancel, especially if the terms are not clear from the outset.

But you have to act. From the moment you receive your policy documents, the clock starts ticking. Ten to thirty days can go fast. That is why I am devoting an entire chapter to this. It is up to you to seek out resources to explore, compare, and verify your policy. LIR is here to empower you in this process. I will shed more light on the ease of the process in a later chapter, so keep reading!

Unpacking Complex Policies: Legalese and Jargon

Having a consumer advocate partner in the free review period is important because life insurance policies are notoriously difficult to read. Filled with legalese, technical terms, and dense clauses, they can leave even savvy consumers confused. Important provisions like premium schedules, exclusions, current rates vs policy guarantees, and riders might be buried in sections that are hard to decipher. This complexity often leads consumers to accept policies without fully understanding them.

Take, for example, the "flexible premiums" clause in many universal life policies. While this feature might sound appealing, the actual implications are often hidden in the fine print. "Flexible" might mean that skipping a payment could reduce your cash value or even lead to policy lapse if not carefully managed. Similarly, a rider advertised as "living benefits" might come with restrictions or conditions that make it less beneficial than it appears.

The free look period gives you the time to carefully dissect your policy's language. Here's how you can approach this process:

- **Seek Independent Advice:** Consult with an expert to clarify ambiguous terms or features.
- **Highlight Key Sections:** Focus on premiums, benefits, current rates, and any clauses that seem unclear.
- **Ask Questions:** Reach out to your agent or broker for clarification, but don't rely solely on their interpretation, independent verification is crucial.

This period is not just a luxury, it's a necessity to ensure you fully understand what you're committing to. The complexity of policy language is one of the primary reasons the free look period was enacted, as it allows consumers to seek expert guidance without the pressure of the initial sales process.

State-Specific Guidelines: How to Find Out What Applies to You

The length and specifics of the free look period vary by state. In most states, the free look period is between 10 and 30 days, starting when you receive your policy documents. Some states also have longer periods for seniors. Understanding the nuances of your state's regulations can help you make the most of this crucial time frame.

Here's how to determine the details for your policy:

1. **Check Your Policy Documents:** The free look period should be explicitly mentioned in the introductory sections or a separate notice. Also, note that some insurance companies offer more time than the state requires, so be sure to check your specific documents.

2. **Ask Your Agent or Broker:** Request confirmation of the free look period's duration and the date it begins.
3. **Research Your State's Regulations:** Visit your state's Department of Insurance website for specific rules and requirements regarding the free look period.

Knowing how long you have and when the period begins ensures you can take full advantage of this provision. Don't hesitate to ask your agent, broker, or financial advisor directly, it's your right to know.

The Legal Perspective: A Shield for Your Rights

From a legal standpoint, the free look period is a critical consumer protection. James explains, "This provision allows policyholders to cancel their contracts without penalty, giving them a rare second chance in a process that is otherwise binding. It's one of the few times in the insurance world where the consumer holds the upper hand."

The free look period safeguards your rights in several ways:

- **Full Refund Guarantee:** If you cancel during the free look period, you're entitled to a full refund of any premiums paid.
- **No Questions Asked:** Insurers cannot penalize you for canceling, regardless of your reasons.
- **Legal Recourse:** If an insurer or agent fails to honor the free look period, you have grounds for a formal complaint or legal action.

This protection levels the playing field, giving consumers the time and space to make decisions free from pressure or manipulation. Without it, consumers could be locked into long-term financial commitments they don't fully understand.

Why Agents Rarely Mention the Free Look Period

While agents are legally required to inform you about the free look period, it's often downplayed or glossed over during the sales process. Here's why: agents see the sale as complete once you sign the contract. The free look period represents a risk to their bottom line, they don't want you to use it, and some may not fully understand how it works themselves.

Think about when you buy a brand new car. If there is a problem with the car or want to understand if something is covered under the warranty, you will not get clear answers from your salesperson. They would simply refer you to the service department. After all, they just spotted a hot prospect on the lot.

Life insurance sales professionals are the same way. They want to make a sale and move on to the next. But there are deeper reasons too. Here's why they might avoid emphasizing the free look period:

- **Sales-Driven Mindset:** They prioritize volume (remember those sales quotas and contests) over long-term relationships.
- **Fear of Scrutiny:** Encouraging clients to closely examine their policies increases the likelihood of cancellations or renegotiations, which they want to avoid.
- **Knowledge Gaps:** Some of them, especially those new to the industry, may not fully grasp the implications of the free look period or its importance to consumers.

Understanding these dynamics reinforces why it's crucial to take control of the free look period yourself. It's a safeguard that puts the power back in your hands, even if your agent isn't eager to highlight it.

Why LifeInsuranceReview.com (LIR) Is Your Best Ally

Navigating the free look period can feel overwhelming, but you don't have to do it alone. At LifeInsuranceReview.com, we specialize in helping consumers understand their policies and make informed decisions. Our process is designed to empower you, ensuring that your life insurance policy serves your best interests, not someone else's bottom line.

By leveraging the free look period, you gain the time and space to make thoughtful, informed decisions. Whether it's uncovering hidden costs, clarifying complex terms, or identifying better options, this critical window gives you the control you deserve.

The free look period is more than a consumer right, it's your chance to ensure your life insurance policy is the best total value for you. Take full advantage of it, and you'll be well on your way to securing the protection and peace of mind you deserve.

How to Use the Free Look Period Effectively

Making the most of the free look period requires a proactive approach. Here's a step-by-step guide to ensure you maximize this critical time frame:

1. **Engage a Trusted Expert Who Is A Fiduciary:** Services like ours (LifeInsuranceReview.com) can provide a comprehensive evaluation of your policy during the free look period. Our

independent review process focuses on your best interest, not the life insurance sales professional's agenda.

2. **Compare Options:** Use this time to explore alternative policies and confirm that your current choice offers the best value.
3. **Verify Details:** Check all aspects of the policy and presented illustrations, including premiums, benefits, exclusions, and riders. Ensure they align with what you were promised during the sales process.
4. **Ask Questions:** Contact your life insurance sales professional for clarification on anything unclear, but always seek independent verification.
5. **Take Action:** If you decide the policy isn't right for you, notify the insurer in writing via email before the free look period expires. Retain documentation of your cancellation request for your records.

CHAPTER EIGHT

COMMON PITFALLS AND HIDDEN COSTS IN LIFE INSURANCE POLICIES

Do you know the difference between education and experience? Education is when you read the fine print; experience is what you get when you don't.

– **Pete Seeger,** American singer-songwriter and musician

When it comes to life insurance, the devil is in the details. What seems like a straightforward policy in the agent's office, can be riddled with exclusions, hidden costs, and restrictive waiting periods. These pitfalls, often buried in the fine print, can significantly impact your coverage and its value to you and your family. Understanding these potential traps is crucial to ensuring that your life insurance policy meets your needs without any unpleasant surprises. In this chapter we will help you understand the hidden dangers that you need to be on the lookout for so you will not fall prey to common pitfalls.

The Small Print That Could Cost You: Exclusions, Hidden Costs, and Waiting Periods

Exclusions: What's Not Covered?

Exclusions are specific conditions or circumstances under which the insurance company will not pay out the policy's benefits. While exclusions are a standard feature in most life insurance policies, they can vary widely between providers and policy types. Common exclusions include:

- **Suicide Clause:** Most policies have a suicide clause that denies benefits if the policyholder dies by suicide within the first two years of coverage.
- **Risky Activities:** If the insured engages in high-risk hobbies or occupations, such as skydiving or scuba diving, the policy may exclude coverage for deaths resulting from those activities.
- **Acts of War or Terrorism:** Many policies will not pay out if the insured's death is related to war or acts of terrorism, especially for those in the military or high-risk regions.
- **Foreign Residency Exclusion:** This applies if the insured person resides permanently or for an extended period in a foreign country that is deemed high-risk or excluded by the policy.
- **Pre-existing Health Conditions:** Some policies may exclude coverage for deaths related to pre-existing conditions that were not disclosed during the application process.

Understanding exclusions is critical to evaluating whether a policy truly meets your needs. Carefully review these sections to ensure that the circumstances most relevant to your life are covered.

Hidden Costs: The Quiet Drain on Your Policy's Value

Life insurance policies often come with costs that are not immediately apparent during the sales process. These costs can erode the value of your policy over time, particularly for permanent policies with cash value components. Here are some common hidden costs, most of which increase every year:

- **Policy Administration Fees:** These are ongoing charges for managing the policy. While they may seem minor, they can add up over the years.
- **Cost of Insurance (COI):** This fee covers the actual cost of providing life insurance coverage and typically increases as you age. In cash value policies, COI can significantly reduce the growth of your cash value.
- **Surrender Charges:** If you cancel your policy early, you may face steep surrender charges, particularly in the first 10 years.
- **Rider Costs:** Having or adding riders, such as disability waivers or accelerated death benefits, often comes with additional costs.

To avoid surprises, ask your life insurance sales professional or insurer directly for a detailed breakdown of all costs associated with the policy. Review annual statements to monitor how these costs impact your policy's value over time. In addition, one of the most helpful reports to generate is the internal rate of return (IRR) report.

Waiting Periods: Delayed Benefits When You Need Them Most Many life insurance policies include waiting periods during which certain benefits are not available. These waiting periods can range from months to years, depending on the policy type and provider. For example:

- **Living Benefits like Long Term Care or Critical, Chronic, and Terminal Illness:** These often have elimination periods (waiting periods) before any benefits are paid. It's crucial to thoroughly review the policy's specific terms and conditions, including how this benefit is calculated, and what specific services it covers.
- **Guaranteed Issue Policies:** These policies, often marketed to individuals with significant health issues, typically have a 2 to 3-year waiting period before full death benefits are payable. If the insured dies during this period, the beneficiary may only receive a refund of premiums paid.
- **Contestability Period:** Most policies include a two-year contestability period, during which the insurer can investigate claims and deny benefits if they find material misrepresentations on the application.

While waiting periods are standard in the industry, it's important to understand their implications. For individuals with urgent life insurance needs, these delays could leave loved ones financially vulnerable at a critical time.

Why You Really Need to Explore, Compare, and Verify

The life insurance market is vast, with policies varying significantly in terms of cost, coverage, and conditions. This variability makes it essential to take a methodical approach to selecting a policy:

1. **Explore Options:** Don't settle for the first policy you're offered. Take the time to explore different providers and policy types. Research each company's reputation and financial stability using tools like the Comdex score.

2. **Compare Policies:** Evaluate policies side by side to understand how they differ in terms of premiums, benefits, exclusions, and fees. Pay attention to the fine print, as even seemingly minor differences can have significant long-term implications.
3. **Verify Details:** Don't rely solely on the life insurance sale professional's explanations. Review the policy documents thoroughly, and consult an independent expert to ensure you fully understand what you're committing to.

The ability to explore, compare, and verify is especially important when you consider the subtle ways policies can be designed to prioritize the insurer's profits over your needs. By taking control of this process, you can ensure that your policy aligns with your financial goals and provides meaningful protection for your family.

The Importance of Not Being Sold

One of the most significant pitfalls in the life insurance industry is the sales-driven approach that many life insurance sale professionals adopt. This sales focus mentality often leads to policies that are more about meeting sales goals than meeting your needs. The fine print in these policies can have life-changing consequences, particularly if exclusions, increasing fees, or waiting periods limit their effectiveness.

Consider this: a policy that looks affordable on the surface might have escalating premiums tied to age or fees that drain its cash value over time. If you were "sold" on the benefits without being fully informed of the costs and its limitations, you could find yourself stuck with a policy that fails to deliver when it matters most.

The key to avoiding this trap is empowerment. When you're informed about how policies work and what to look for, you're less likely to fall victim to pressure-based sales tactics or misleading pitches. Instead of being sold, you can make a deliberate choice that prioritizes your needs.

Comdex Scores: A Key Tool for Evaluating Insurers

One often overlooked aspect of life insurance selection is the financial stability of the insurer. The Comdex score is a valuable tool for assessing this stability. It consolidates ratings from major agencies, such as A.M. Best, Moody's, and Standard & Poor's, into a single percentile ranking. The higher the Comdex score, the stronger the insurer's financial position.

Why does this matter? An insurer's financial health directly impacts its ability to pay claims, particularly in times of economic downturn or increased claim activity. Choosing a company with a high Comdex score can increase the likelihood that your policy's benefits will be available when your family needs them most.

When evaluating policies, always ask about the insurer's Comdex score. It's a straightforward way to verify the company's reliability and protect your investment.

Real-World Impacts of the Fine Print

The consequences of overlooking exclusions, hidden costs, and waiting periods can be devastating. Not in a "that's a bummer" way but in a negative life-changing way. They can negate the whole reason why you bought life insurance in the first place and represent the worst-case scenario that you were actively trying to avoid. Here are some real-world examples:

- **The Unexpected Exclusion:** A policyholder after being covered for less than one year moves to another country to retire and then later filed a claim for a chronic illness. The insurer denies the claim because of a policy exclusion that was never properly explained or highlighted during the original sales process. Consequently, the family finds themselves financially devastated, a direct result of inadequate disclosure.
- **The Costly Fees:** A couple invested in a universal life policy, counting on its cash value to grow significantly. However, about six years in, they discovered a harsh reality: lower interest rate credits and rising policy expenses were eroding their cash value much faster than the initial illustration showed. This left them with far less money than they'd anticipated. By the time they realized the problem, steep surrender charges made it costly to now switch to a new better designed policy, costing them six years of opportunity cost.
- **The Waiting Period Dilemma:** An individual battling cancer relied on their life insurance policy's critical illness rider for financial support. Yet, when they filed a claim, the payout was unexpectedly low. To make matters worse, the rider's accelerated benefit also drastically reduced their policy's death benefit. This left the client feeling profoundly frustrated, believing they weren't given complete or accurate information from the start.

I hope these scenarios bring home the importance of thoroughly understanding your policy before committing. The free look period, discussed in the previous chapter, is an invaluable tool for identifying these pitfalls before it's too late.

Why Some Policies May Not Pay Out When You Need Them Most

Life insurance is often purchased with the assurance that it will provide financial security at critical moments. However, the unfortunate reality is that not all policies fulfill this promise. James highlights this stark truth, explaining, "It's not just about buying life insurance, it's about buying the right life insurance. Otherwise, you may find out too late that your policy doesn't deliver when you need it most."

Understanding Policy Payout Failures

There are several reasons why life insurance policies fail to pay out as expected. These include both intentional and unintentional factors, often buried in the fine print or overlooked during the sales process:

1. **Material Misrepresentation During Application**
   One of the most common reasons for claim denial is material misrepresentation. If the insurer discovers that the policyholder provided inaccurate or incomplete information during the application process, they may refuse to pay the claim. This could include anything from undisclosed health conditions to understated lifestyle risks like smoking or high-risk hobbies.

2. **Failure to Disclose Medical Conditions**
   Even minor omissions, such as failing to disclose occasional treatment for high blood pressure, can lead to a claim being denied. The application process is legally binding, and any discrepancies between the application and medical records can create grounds for rejection.
3. **Lapsed Policies Due to Missed Premiums**
   Policies lapse when premiums are not paid on time, and many policyholders are unaware of the grace periods or reinstatement options. A policy lapse can render a contract void, leaving beneficiaries with nothing.
4. **Contestability Period Complications**
   During the first two years of most life insurance policies, the insurer can contest claims for any reason. Even if a claim is legitimate, the contestability period often invites additional scrutiny, creating delays or outright denials.
5. **Excluded Causes of Death**
   Policies often have exclusions for specific causes of death, such as suicide within the first two years, acts of war, or death resulting from high-risk activities. If the insured passes away under one of these conditions, the claim will not be honored.

Common Reasons for Policy Denials

Based on years of experience doing life insurance reviews for both professionals and consumers, here are additional scenarios that commonly lead to denials:

1. **Inconsistent Documentation**
   One frequent issue I see is documentation that doesn't match up. If application details, beneficiary information, or medical records are inconsistent, insurers may reject claims outright or demand further verification.
2. **Outdated Beneficiary Designations**
   Many policyholders forget to update their beneficiaries after major life events like marriage, divorce, or the birth of a child. This can lead to legal disputes or payouts being made to unintended recipients.
3. **Misunderstood Riders**
   Riders, such as those offering accelerated death benefits, often come with conditions that aren't clearly communicated during the sales process. Policyholders may assume they're covered in certain scenarios, only to discover that stringent qualifications exclude their situation.
4. **Administrative Errors**
   Errors during policy setup, such as incorrect premium calculations or misapplied payments can lead to policies lapsing without the policyholder realizing it.

How to Avoid These Hidden Traps

Avoiding these pitfalls requires careful attention at every stage of the life insurance process—from application to ongoing management. Here are some actionable steps to ensure your policy delivers when it matters most:

1. **Disclose Everything Honestly**
   Be completely transparent during the application process. If in doubt, err on the side of over-disclosure. It's better to provide more information than necessary than to risk a denial based on perceived omissions.
2. **Understand the Fine Print**
   Take the time to read and understand every aspect of your policy. Pay close attention to exclusions, conditions, and premium schedules. If anything is unclear, ask for clarification from a trusted expert, not just your agent.
3. **Regularly Update Beneficiary Information**
   Ensure your policy reflects your current circumstances. Review and update beneficiary designations after major life events to avoid complications down the road.
4. **Monitor Your Policy's Status**
   Keep track of premium payments and ensure that your policy is in good standing. Set reminders for due dates and confirm payment receipt with the insurer.
5. **Seek Expert Review**
   Engage a service like LIR to conduct an independent evaluation of your policy. Our comprehensive 28-point review can uncover hidden dangers and ensure your policy meets your needs.

How LifeInsuranceReview.com (LIR) Protects You

LIR's mission is to empower you with clarity and confidence in your life insurance decisions. Through the 28-point review process, we scrutinize policies for potential pitfalls that could undermine their value. This thorough evaluation includes:

1. **Policy Structure Analysis**
   Are the policy's terms consistent with the policyholder's goals? LIR evaluates whether the coverage type (e.g., term, whole, universal) is appropriate for the client's needs.
2. **Exclusions Review**
   Every exclusion is carefully examined to ensure that there are no unexpected limitations that could affect payout eligibility.
3. **Rider Evaluation**
   Optional riders are analyzed for value and necessity, ensuring they provide meaningful benefits without excessive cost.
4. **Premium Sustainability**
   LIR assesses whether premium payments are manageable long-term, particularly for permanent policies with variable components.
5. **Benefit Adequacy**
   Does the death benefit adequately address the policyholder's financial goals, such as income replacement or estate planning? LIR ensures that coverage levels meet these objectives.
6. **Fee Transparency**
   All associated fees, including administration charges and cost-of-insurance rates, are identified and explained.
7. **Claims Process Clarity**
   LIR evaluates the claims process to ensure it is straightforward and transparent, reducing potential obstacles for beneficiaries.

Why a Second Opinion Matters

When it comes to life insurance, even minor oversights can have significant consequences. LIR's 28-point review process ensures that no detail is overlooked, providing peace of mind and financial security.

James concludes, "A second opinion isn't just valuable, it's essential. With so much at stake, you need to know that your policy will deliver when you need it most."

LIR is here to ensure that no one has to navigate this process alone. Our reviews aren't just about policies, they're about empowering people to buy life insurance with clear confidence.

Through our meticulous approach,

LIR helps consumers avoid the pitfalls of poorly designed policies, ensuring that their investments in life insurance truly serve their intended purpose.

Checklist to Review with your Life Insurance Sales Professionals

What to Double-Check Before Signing a Life Insurance Policy:

- ☐ **Annual Fees and Charges**
  Identify all fees associated with the policy, including administrative fees, rider costs, and surrender charges.
- ☐ **Premium Structure**
  Confirm whether premiums are fixed or variable and whether they could increase over time.

- ☐ **Coverage Amount**
  Ensure the death benefit is sufficient to meet your family's financial needs, such as covering debts, replacing income, or funding future expenses.
- ☐ **Policy Type**
  Verify that the policy type (term, whole, universal, or variable) aligns with your goals and budget.
- ☐ **Policy Riders**
  Double-check any additional riders (e.g., disability waiver, critical illness benefits, Long-Term Care) to see if they add value or unnecessary costs.
- ☐ **Policy Illustration**
  For permanent policies, review to clearly understand the final illustration that spells out the fine important details of what is guaranteed and non-guaranteed
- ☐ **Renewability and Convertibility**
  For term policies, verify whether the policy is renewable or convertible and under what conditions.
- ☐ **Beneficiary Designations**
  Confirm that all beneficiary details are accurate and reflect your current wishes.

CHAPTER NINE

LIFE CHANGES, SO SHOULD YOUR LIFE INSURANCE

Life moves pretty fast. If you don't stop and look around once in a while, you could miss it.
– **Ferris Bueller** (from "Ferris Bueller's Day Off")

If your life is anything like mine, it is moving fast. One minute it's college. Blink your eyes and you're starting a family. Blink again and you are launching a new business with your partners. The fact is that life insurance can feel like something that you check off your list and never have to worry about again. Not true, life insurance isn't a one-and-done decision.

Just like your life evolves, so do your financial responsibilities and protection needs. The policy you bought when you were fresh out of college may not fit the life you're living now. Marriage, children, homeownership, business ventures—these milestones significantly impact your financial priorities and necessitate adjustments to your life insurance coverage.

However, the reality is that life insurance agents or brokers rarely review policies with their clients after the initial sale. This chapter will delve into why that is, how major life events should influence your coverage, and the steps you can take to ensure your policy evolves with your life.

The Importance of Regular Policy Reviews

Life is dynamic, and your insurance coverage has to reflect that. A regular review of your life insurance policy is essential to make sure it continues to meet your needs. This process can reveal whether your coverage is adequate, identify outdated beneficiaries, and uncover opportunities to optimize costs.

Why Review Your Policy?

1. **Adequacy of Coverage**: As your financial responsibilities grow, so does the need for a higher death benefit. For instance, a policy that once covered your personal debts may now need to account for a mortgage, childcare, or college tuition.
2. **Outdated Beneficiary Designations**: Major life events like marriage or divorce often necessitate changes to your policy's beneficiaries. Failure to update this information can lead to unintended outcomes and headaches (or worse, heartaches) for the people you leave behind.
3. **Policy Performance**: If you have a permanent policy with a cash value component, periodic reviews can help you track its performance. Underperforming investments or rising costs of insurance may necessitate adjustments.

Why You Probably Won't Get a Call From the Agent or Broker

As we discussed in Chapter 5, the life insurance industry is structured to prioritize new sales over ongoing policy servicing. Agents and brokers are incentivized most to sell policies, not to maintain them. Commissions, bonuses, and extra financial incentives are paid mostly in the first one to two years of your policy. Once a policy is sold, agents and brokers often move on to the next prospect, leaving clients to navigate changes in their lives without the same level of attention and professional guidance.

Commission-Driven Sales Model

Life Insurance Sales professionals earn their living from sales, not from servicing policies. This model disincentivizes follow-up services like periodic policy reviews. Their business relies heavily on prospecting for new clients. Unlike financial advisors who can charge for ongoing portfolio management, life insurance agents and brokers typically don't have similar business models that include frequent product reviews. And if they do, they don't typically discuss alternative product options like new, competitive life policies, benefits, features, etc.

Lack of Training and Resources

Many agents lack the training or resources to conduct thorough policy reviews. Their focus is often on selling specific products rather than understanding the nuances of existing policies or how life changes affect coverage needs. In addition, they only know what they are trained to know and do not have the time and focus to look outside to learn new policy options from different insurance companies. Mainly, if there's not a worthwhile financial incentive, the agents and brokers are simply not motivated. As a result, they may not have the expertise to offer meaningful advice beyond the initial sale.

Life Events That Necessitate Policy Updates

Certain milestones in life significantly impact your financial obligations and risk profile. Here's how major life events can necessitate changes to your life insurance policy:

Marriage

Getting married often means combining finances and sharing responsibilities with your spouse. Your life insurance should reflect this new dynamic by ensuring that your partner is financially protected in case of your untimely death. Consider increasing your coverage to account for shared debts/financial responsibilities, such as a mortgage or joint credit cards, and updating your beneficiary designations to include your spouse.

Children

The arrival of a child is one of the most significant reasons to reevaluate your life insurance coverage. The financial cost of raising a child—factoring in education, healthcare, and day-to-day expenses—can easily exceed hundreds of thousands of dollars. Life insurance ensures that your children will be provided for if you're no longer there to support them.

Options to consider include:

- Increasing your death benefit to cover future educational expenses.

- Adding riders that provide additional coverage for your children or include benefits like guaranteed insurability.

Homeownership

Buying a home is a significant financial commitment. Your life insurance policy should include enough coverage to pay off the mortgage, ensuring that your family can remain in the home without financial strain.

Business Ventures

Starting or expanding a business brings unique financial risks and opportunities. Life insurance can play a critical role in ensuring business continuity. For example:

- **Buy-Sell Agreements:** Life insurance can fund buy-sell agreements, allowing surviving business partners to buy out your share of the company.
- **Key Person Insurance:** If you're a key figure in your business, life insurance can provide the financial resources needed to hire and train a replacement.

Why Life Changes Necessitate Professional Reviews

While you can take some steps to evaluate your policy on your own, a professional review is invaluable. Experts like those of us at LifeInsuranceReview.com bring the experience and tools needed to uncover hidden issues and optimize your coverage. We understand financial, tax, and estate planning. We know clearly how life insurance can fit best into your plan.

LIR is unique because we take an in-house team approach of professionals from estate planning attorneys to CPAs, CFPs, CLUs, and life insurance analysts together under one roof, all working collaboratively for you. It's why we are trusted by both professionals and consumers alike.

The Real-World Impacts of Neglected Reviews

Let me share a recent circumstance to bring my point home. A client came to us after their spouse passed away. They hadn't updated their life insurance policy in over 15 years. The primary beneficiary was still listed as an ex-spouse, creating a legal nightmare for the family. This could have been avoided with a simple review.

James: The Legal Perspective on Policy Reviews

James emphasizes the legal implications of neglecting updates. "Failing to review and update your policy can have serious consequences, including disputes over beneficiary designations or inadequate coverage. These are issues that no family should face during an already difficult time."

How to Conduct a Life Insurance Review

A comprehensive policy review involves several steps:

1. **Assess Your Current Coverage**: Start by understanding what your policy covers, including death benefits, exclusions, and cash value performance (if applicable).
2. **Evaluate Life Changes**: Consider how your circumstances have changed since you purchased the policy.

3. **Make Necessary Updates**: Update beneficiaries, adjust coverage levels, or modify policy features as needed.

How LifeInsuranceReview.com (LIR) Can Help

At LIR, we specialize in helping consumers navigate the complexities of life insurance. Our services are designed to:

- **Uncover Hidden Issues**: We identify outdated beneficiaries, insufficient coverage, and underperforming policies.
- **Provide Independent Council**: As fiduciary-focused advisors, we prioritize your needs over sales goals.
- **Empower You to Make Informed Decisions**: We provide the tools, resources, and expertise you need to ensure your policy clearly provides you with the best value for your planning.

By taking a proactive approach to policy reviews, we help clients avoid the pitfalls of outdated coverage and ensure that their life insurance evolves alongside their lives.

Life Insurance: Not a One-and-Done Process

Life insurance is a living financial tool, meant to grow and adapt alongside your life. However, when policies remain static while your circumstances change, the result can be devastating: either underinsurance that leaves loved ones financially vulnerable or overinsurance that drains your resources unnecessarily.

James emphasizes this point: "Outdated policies can cost you more than money—they can cost you security and peace of mind."

This section explores the consequences of neglecting your policy, real-life stories of clients who benefited from timely reviews, and practical guidelines to ensure your coverage stays relevant.

The Risks of Outdated Policies

Outdated life insurance policies are more common than most people realize, and they often go unnoticed until it's too late. Whether it's insufficient coverage, unnecessary riders, or overinflated premiums, these issues can undermine the financial protection you intend to secure for your loved ones.

Underinsurance: Leaving Loved Ones Vulnerable

Life changes—such as having children, buying a home, or starting a business—can significantly increase your financial obligations. If your policy's death benefit doesn't keep pace, your family could be left struggling to cover essential expenses.

For example:

- A family with young children may rely on a sole breadwinner's income. If the breadwinner's life insurance policy hasn't been updated since their single days, the death benefit may fall short of covering childcare, education, and living expenses.
- A homeowner might still have the same policy they purchased before taking on a mortgage. Should they pass away, their family could face losing the home due to an insufficient payout.

Overinsurance: Paying for What You Don't Need

On the flip side, overinsurance is a costly issue for those whose circumstances have changed but whose policies remain the same. For instance:

- A retiree with no dependents may no longer need the high death benefit they purchased decades earlier but continues to pay inflated premiums.
- A business owner who sold their company might still be maintaining a key person insurance policy that is no longer relevant, wasting thousands of dollars annually.

Unnecessary Riders

Riders can add value, but they can also increase premiums unnecessarily when circumstances change. For example, a waiver of premium rider might no longer be needed if the insured has substantial savings, yet its cost remains baked into the policy.

Why Periodic Reviews Are Essential

Periodic reviews ensure that your policy remains a valuable financial asset rather than a dormant liability. Here are key benefits of conducting regular reviews:

1. **Aligning Coverage with Life Changes**: Life insurance should evolve with your financial responsibilities, whether that means increasing coverage for growing families or reducing it during retirement.
2. **Eliminating Redundancies**: Reviews can identify unnecessary riders or policies, helping you save on premiums.

3. **Optimizing Cash Value Performance**: For permanent policies, regular reviews allow you to monitor cash value growth and adjust contributions if needed.

Guidelines for Reviewing Your Policy

To maintain relevant and effective coverage, it's crucial to review your life insurance policy regularly. Below are guidelines for when and how to conduct these reviews:

How Often Should You Review Your Policy?

1. **Annually**: A yearly check-in ensures your policy aligns with your current financial goals and obligations.
2. **After Major Life Events**: Significant milestones such as marriage, divorce, childbirth, home purchase, or retirement warrant an immediate review.
3. **Every Three to Five Years at least**: Even without major changes, a three to five year review is recommended to account for shifts in market conditions, health, or financial needs.

What to Look For During a Review

1. **Coverage Adequacy**: Does the death benefit cover your current financial obligations?
2. **Beneficiary Updates**: Are your beneficiaries up to date and reflective of your intentions?
3. **Riders and Features**: Are the riders you're paying for still necessary?
4. **Policy Performance**: For cash value policies, is the growth meeting your expectations?

5. **Premium Affordability**: Are the premiums sustainable based on your income and financial goals?

How LIR Supports You

At LifeInsuranceReview.com (LIR), we understand that life insurance is more than a policy—it's a promise to protect your loved ones. Our process is designed to ensure that this promise is fulfilled, no matter how your life changes.

Comprehensive 28-Point Review

Our 28-point review process evaluates every aspect of your policy, from beneficiary designations to cash value performance. Here's what we look for:

- **Death Benefit Adequacy**: Is the coverage sufficient to meet your family's needs?
- **Exclusion Clarity**: Are there any conditions that could prevent a payout?
- **Fee Transparency**: Are hidden costs or scheduled rising costs eroding your policy's value?
- **Rider Relevance**: Are you paying for features you no longer need?

Empowering You to Make Informed Decisions

Unlike sales-driven agents, brokers, or financial advisors, our focus is on empowering you to make informed decisions. We provide transparent, unbiased counsel tailored to your unique circumstances.

Life Insurance Should Grow with You

Life insurance is a dynamic asset that should grow and adapt as your life evolves. Through periodic reviews, you can ensure that your policy remains aligned with your needs, providing both financial security and peace of mind.

Whether you're just starting a family, launching a business, or enjoying retirement, LifeInsuranceReview.com is here to guide you every step of the way. With our expertise, you can navigate life's changes with confidence, knowing that your life insurance is always working in your best interest.

Is it time for a Policy Review?

Check the applicable boxes below:

- ☐ Have you recently been married or divorced?
- ☐ Have you recently changed careers or jobs?
- ☐ Have you recently purchased a property?
- ☐ Have you recently sold a property or business?
- ☐ Have you increased or decreased the number of dependents?
- ☐ Are you planning to retire in the next 5-10 years, or have you recently retired?
- ☐ Has your insurable interest changed or has your health recently declined?
- ☐ Would you like to find out how much the same coverage would cost today?
- ☐ Do you want to learn more or add benefits like Long-Term Care, Disability, or Living Benefits?

- ☐ Has the cash value in your policy not performed as well as you had hoped?
- ☐ Are you planning to take any distributions from your policy's cash value?
- ☐ Do you plan on modifying your premium or coverage, or canceling your policy?
- ☐ Do you want to explore your life or viatical settlement options?
- ☐ Have you reviewed and updated your life insurance policy to align with your estate plan?
- ☐ Has it been over three years since you reviewed your life insurance policy with a professional?

CHAPTER TEN

THE ALTERNATIVE

– Why Term Life Insurance Is Often the Appropriate Choice

The quality of your life is built on the quality of your decisions.

– **Wesam Fawzi,** Strategist on marketing, dynamic business modernization, and leadership performance

When it comes to life insurance, there are decisions that you have to make based on your current situation. These decisions can depend on your life circumstances and your obligations. The choices you make today may not be the same choices you would make in the future when your circumstances have changed. For example, the life insurance choices of a man with a young family may be different from those of a multimillionaire with no dependents.

If you fall into the former category, there is an option that stands out for its simplicity, affordability, and ability to meet the needs of most families: term life insurance. While other types of policies like whole life or universal life may seem appealing due to their added features, the reality is that term life insurance often provides the best value for individuals and families looking for straightforward financial protection. This chapter takes a deep dive into term life insurance, explaining why it is often the smartest choice and outlining the situations where it is best suited.

What Is Term Life Insurance?

Term life insurance is the simplest and most affordable type of life insurance. At its core, it provides coverage for a specified period, or "term," such as 10, 20, 30, up to 40 years. If the policyholder passes away during this term, their beneficiaries receive a death benefit, typically a tax-free lump sum. If the policyholder survives the term, the coverage ends, and no benefit is paid out.

Unlike permanent policies, term life insurance doesn't include savings components, cash value accumulation, or investment features. Its sole purpose is to provide financial protection for a set period, making it a straightforward and highly effective solution for many people.

Key Features of Term Life Insurance

1. **Fixed Premiums**: During the term, premiums remain constant, allowing for predictable budgeting.
2. **Flexible Terms**: Policies are available in varying lengths, typically ranging from 5 to 30 years.
3. **High Coverage, Low Cost**: For the same premium, term life insurance provides significantly higher death benefits compared to permanent policies.

Why Simplicity Matters

One of the primary advantages of term life insurance is its simplicity. Unlike whole or universal life policies, which can be confusing due to their complex structures and multiple components, term life insurance is easy to understand. You pay a premium, and in exchange, your loved ones are protected for a specific period.

This simplicity eliminates the guesswork, ensuring you know exactly what you're paying for and what your family will receive in the event of your passing. It's an insurance product designed to do one thing well: provide financial protection when it's needed most.

Affordability: The Core Advantage

For families looking to maximize their financial resources, term life insurance offers unparalleled affordability. Premiums for term policies are a fraction of those for whole or universal life policies, making it possible to secure substantial coverage without straining your budget.

For example, a healthy 35-year-old might pay $25 a month for a 20-year, $500,000 term policy. In comparison, a permanent policy with the same death benefit could cost upwards of $300 a month. This cost difference allows families to allocate more resources toward other financial goals, such as saving for retirement, paying down debt, or funding a child's educational savings plan.

Breaking Down the Cost Difference

The lower cost of term life insurance is due to its focus on pure protection. Since there's no cash value accumulation or investment component, insurers don't have to account for long-term growth or administrative fees associated with managing those features. As a result, you get more coverage for less money.

Flexibility to Meet Changing Needs

Term life insurance is highly adaptable, making it an excellent choice for individuals whose financial responsibilities change over time. Policies can be tailored to align with specific goals, such as:

1. **Income Replacement**: Providing a financial safety net for dependents if a breadwinner passes away.
2. **Debt Coverage**: Ensuring that outstanding debts, such as mortgages, car loans, or student loans, are paid off.
3. **Childcare and Education Costs**: Covering the cost of raising children and funding their education.

Additionally, many term policies come with options to convert to permanent coverage without requiring a medical exam. This feature can be valuable if your needs change or if you develop health issues that make securing new coverage difficult.

Comparison with Other Types of Life Insurance

Whole Life Insurance

- **Cost**: Whole life policies are significantly more expensive than term policies, often costing 10-15 times more for the same coverage amount.

- **Complexity**: Whole life policies include savings and investment components that can be difficult to understand and manage.
- **Best Use Case**: Whole life insurance is best suited for individuals with long-term estate planning needs or those seeking a financial product that combines insurance and savings.

Universal Life Insurance

- **Flexibility**: Universal life policies offer adjustable premiums and death benefits, but this flexibility comes at a cost.
- **Investment Risk**: These policies often tie cash value growth to market performance, introducing a level of risk not present in term policies.
- **Best Use Case**: Universal life insurance may be appropriate for individuals with complex financial goals and the resources to manage a more expensive and volatile policy.

Why Term Often Wins

For the majority of families, the affordability and straightforward nature of term life insurance make it the clear winner. Permanent policies may offer additional features, but they're often unnecessary for individuals whose primary goal is to provide financial protection during their working years.

When Term Life Insurance Is the Best Choice

There are many situations where term life insurance is the ideal solution:

1. **Young Families**

   For young parents with limited budgets, term life insurance provides affordable coverage to protect their children's future. A

20 or 30 year term policy can ensure that children are cared for until they're financially independent.

2. **Homeowners**
   Homeownership often comes with significant debt in the form of a mortgage. A term policy can be matched to the length of the loan, ensuring that the home remains in the family if the primary income earner passes away.
3. **Business Owners**
   Entrepreneurs often use term life insurance to secure loans or provide key person coverage. These policies offer temporary protection during critical growth periods without the high cost of permanent coverage.
4. **Individuals with Temporary Needs**
   For those with short-term financial obligations, such as caring for an aging parent or funding a child's college education, term life insurance provides targeted coverage without long-term commitments.

How to Maximize the Benefits of Term Life Insurance

Of course, no life insurance policy is perfect for every circumstance. There are considerations that can help you make a term life policy a better fit for your circumstances. To get the most out of your term life insurance policy, it's essential to consider the following factors:

1. **Choose the Right Term Length**
   Select a term that aligns with your financial goals. For example, if your goal is to pay off a 30-year mortgage, a 30-year term policy makes sense.

2. **Buy Sufficient Coverage**
   Calculate the total amount your family would need to cover expenses, debts, and future goals. Don't underestimate your needs—err on the side of caution.
3. **Ask About Living Benefits**
   As the name suggests, these benefits are paid to you while you are living, instead of when you die. They can help cover expenses from critical, chronic, and terminal illness. Common illnesses covered may include stroke, heart attack, and cancer. Living benefits are essentially an advancement of the death benefit that is provided to you tax-free. These living benefits greatly protect your financial plan. You may be surprised to learn that some term policies provide these three living benefits (coverage for chronic, critical, and terminal illness) at no additional cost. Visit the term insurance section of our webpage for more info: https://www.lifeinsurancereview.com/term-life-insurance
4. **Work with an Independent Advisor**
   Independent advisors can help you compare policies from multiple insurers, ensuring you get the best value for your money.
5. **Review Your Policy Periodically**
   Life circumstances change, and your coverage should adapt accordingly. Regular reviews ensure that your policy continues to meet your needs.

Term life insurance offers a simple, affordable, and flexible way to protect your family's financial future. By focusing on what truly matters—providing a safety net for your loved ones—it avoids the complexity and high costs associated with permanent policies. For most individuals and families, term life insurance is the smart choice that delivers peace of mind without breaking the bank.

How to Know When Your Needs Might Outgrow Term Life Insurance

While term life insurance is an excellent option for many, life's changes may eventually necessitate a reevaluation of your coverage. A term policy, designed for temporary protection, might not always suffice as your financial responsibilities evolve. Whether it's the need for lifetime coverage, cash value benefits, or addressing long-term financial goals, understanding when your needs might outgrow term life insurance is crucial.

The options you choose today may be appropriate for your current needs, but may not be appropriate for your future needs. It is important to periodically reevaluate your needs. If you open a business, buy a home, or have a child (or two or three), your obligations will change and your insurance needs will change as well.

Another Dirty Industry Fact: Why Term Life Insurance is Often Not Offered by Agents & Brokers

Despite its affordability and simplicity, term life insurance is frequently overlooked by agents and brokers. The reason? It doesn't pay as well. The commission structure in the life insurance industry heavily favors permanent policies, which generate higher premiums and, in turn, higher commissions for the salesperson.

This means that agents often steer clients toward whole life or universal life because of additional benefits, even when term life insurance would be more appropriate. The industry's sales-driven culture creates a conflict of interest, where the client's best interest may take a back seat to the agent's financial incentives.

Another thing to consider, agents and brokers are rarely incentivized to revisit a term policy they've sold because there's little ongoing commission to be made. That's why we emphasize the need for independent reviews to ensure your coverage continues to align with your goals.

When Term Life Insurance May No Longer Meet Your Needs

1. **The Need for Lifetime Coverage**:
   If you find that your financial obligations extend well beyond the typical 20 or 30 year term lengths, a term policy may leave your family exposed after the coverage ends. Common examples include:
   - **Caring for a Special Needs Dependent**: Lifetime financial protection may be required to provide ongoing care.
   - **Estate Planning**: Term life policies don't offer the liquidity needed to address estate taxes or create intergenerational wealth.
2. **The Desire for Cash Value**:
   While term life insurance excels at providing straightforward death benefits, it lacks a savings or investment component. For

those looking to build cash value over time, permanent policies like whole life or indexed universal life might be more suitable.

3. **Health Changes or Aging**:
   As you grow older, renewing or purchasing a new term policy can become prohibitively expensive. Health changes may also make it difficult to secure new coverage. This is where conversion options—if available—can be invaluable.
4. **Significant Wealth Accumulation or Complex Financial Goals**:
   High-net-worth individuals often require life insurance policies tailored to tax efficiency, wealth transfer, or business continuity planning. These goals are typically better addressed by permanent policies.

The Role of LifeInsuranceReview.com (LIR) in Navigating These Decisions

LIR specializes in helping clients determine whether their current coverage still matches their evolving needs. By offering unbiased, fiduciary-focused counsel, LIR helps you make informed decisions based on your unique financial situation—not the commission-driven motivations of an agent or broker.

How LIR Supports Clients

1. **Unbiased Needs Assessment**:
   LIR starts by understanding your financial obligations, future goals, and current coverage. This includes an analysis of whether your term policy can be adjusted or converted to meet changing needs.

2. **Policy Reviews:**
   LIR's 28-point review process uncovers potential gaps, hidden costs, or limitations in your existing policy. For term policies nearing expiration, this includes exploring conversion options and evaluating whether additional coverage is required.
3. **Scenario Planning:**
   LIR walks clients through potential life changes—retirement, estate planning, or new business ventures—and provides tailored recommendations for coverage.

Comparing Term vs. Permanent Policies for Evolving Needs

Feature	Term Life Insurance	Permanent Life Insurance
Cost	Low	High
Duration	10-40 years max (depends on current age)	Lifetime
Cash Value	None	Yes
Riders	Limited, such as Disability, Critical, Chronic, and Terminal Illness	Broader, including tax and estate planning benefits.
Flexibility	Limited	Broad (customizable options)
Best For	Temporary needs (mortgage, income replacement)	Long-term goals (estate planning, intergenerational wealth)

How to Know If It's Time to Transition

Making the decision to transition from term to permanent coverage requires careful consideration. Here are some signs that it may be time to consider this option:

1. **Your Financial Obligations Have Increased**:
   If you've taken on additional responsibilities, such as supporting aging parents or funding a child's extended education, your term policy may no longer provide sufficient coverage.
2. **You're Approaching Retirement**:
   As you prepare to leave the workforce, permanent coverage can help supplement retirement income or ensure liquidity for estate taxes.
3. **You Want to Leave a Legacy**:
   Permanent policies are uniquely suited for creating financial legacies, whether through charitable contributions or intergenerational wealth transfers.
4. **You're Facing Health Challenges**:
   Health changes can make new coverage prohibitively expensive. Converting an existing term policy to permanent coverage ensures continued protection without the need for a medical exam.

Maximizing the Benefits of Term Life Insurance

Maximizing the benefits of term life insurance requires thoughtful planning and proactive management. Even if term coverage is the best fit for your current needs, there are strategies to ensure you're getting the most value from your policy.

One key consideration is evaluating conversion options. Many term policies offer the ability to transition to permanent coverage without requiring a medical exam. This feature can be incredibly valuable as your circumstances change, but it's essential to understand the specific terms and deadlines associated with this option. Missing the conversion window could mean losing the chance to secure permanent coverage if your health changes.

Another strategy to maximize term life insurance is layering policies. Instead of depending on a single term policy, you can layer multiple policies with staggered expiration dates. For example, you might have one policy to cover your mortgage, another for your children's education, and a third to replace income during your prime earning years. This approach aligns your coverage with specific financial milestones, ensuring that you're neither overinsured or underinsured at any given time.

Consulting an expert can make all the difference. A fiduciary-focused advisor (like LIR) can review your policies, help you optimize coverage, and ensure your insurance aligns with your broader financial goals. With their guidance, you can navigate the complexities of term life insurance confidently, making adjustments as your needs change over time.

Final Thoughts on Term Life

While term life insurance is an excellent solution for many families, life's complexities often require more nuanced planning. By working with trusted experts like LIR, you can ensure that your coverage evolves with your needs, providing peace of mind and financial security for years to come.

Whether you're transitioning to a permanent policy or maximizing the benefits of term coverage, the key is staying proactive and informed. Life changes and so should your life insurance.

CHAPTER ELEVEN

HOW TO SPOT RED FLAGS AND PROTECT YOURSELF

We learned the hard way that you can't just trust one person's opinion, no matter how nice they seem. Get a second, and even a third opinion from people who aren't trying to sell you something.

— **Carlos G,** Advocate for Independent Review

Life insurance is a critical financial tool, but the buying process is full of pitfalls that can leave you vulnerable. While the right policy can provide invaluable security, the wrong policy can create financial strain or fail to meet your needs when you need it most. Recognizing the red flags during the buying process is essential to protecting yourself from being misled or sold a product that doesn't align with your goals.

In this chapter, we'll examine the most common warning signs that a policy might not be in your best interest, and provide actionable steps to ensure you make an informed decision.

Pressure-Based Sales Tactics

One of the most immediate red flags in the life insurance sales process is pressure-based tactics. If an agent or broker is rushing you to make a decision, it's time to hit pause.

REMEMBER: Life insurance is too important to be a rushed decision. If someone is pressuring you to sign on the dotted line, it's more about their sales goals than your needs.

How to Spot Pressure-Based Sales Tactics.

As we have discussed, just discussing life insurance can heighten emotions. And emotions can cloud your thinking. Here are some sales tactics that you can be on the lookout for. If you experience them, stop, take a breath, and ask for more time to consider your options.

1. **Urgent Deadlines**
   Some agents may claim that a policy offer is only available for a limited time, creating a false sense of urgency. They might say things like, "This rate is only good if you sign soon." However, life insurance policies are not seasonal sales items; you should have ample time to review your options.
2. **Fear-Based Messaging**
   Agents may exploit your fears by emphasizing worst-case scenarios without providing clear, unbiased information. Statements like, "What happens to your family if you die tomorrow?" are meant to evoke emotion rather than encourage thoughtful decision-making.

3. **Overwhelming You with Information**
   Another tactic is to flood you with complex policy details and technical jargon, making it harder for you to ask critical questions. You may rush to accept the policy just to get out of the uncomfortable situation.

How to Protect Yourself

My recommendation is to not make any final decisions during the sales meeting, especially if you experience any of these pressure-based sales tactics. Allow yourself ample time after the sales meeting, to consider your options, in order to avoid making a commitment you might regret later. It is perfectly acceptable to inform the agent/broker that you need to "think about it".

- **Take Your Time**: A trustworthy advisor will respect your need to consider your options and ask questions.
- **Get a Second Opinion**: Services like LifeInsuranceReview.com can help you evaluate whether the policy aligns with your needs.

If the salesperson objects, empower yourself to:

- **Set Boundaries**: You're the one making the decision, the power is with you, not the agent or broker.

Complex Products That Seem Too Good to Be True

Another red flag is the promise of a product that appears to solve all your problems and answer your every need. Every life insurance product involves trade-offs in regards to its pricing. It is important to understand what those trade-offs are.

As my partner James warns, "If it sounds too good to be true, it probably is. Life insurance products that promise high returns, low premiums, and maximum flexibility often come with hidden caveats that can cost you later."

Examples of Complex Products

1. **Indexed Universal Life (IUL) Policies**
   These policies are often marketed as combining the best features of term and whole life insurance, with cash value growth tied to stock market performance. While they sound attractive, IULs often include caps on returns, high fees, and complex features that can diminish their value. It is also important to note that insurance companies can decide to change their rates and fees from year to year.
2. **Whole Life (WL) Policies**
   Whole Life policies are often presented as bond or savings alternatives, with their cash value growth based on the insurance company's annual declared dividends. However, it's crucial to understand that these policies inherently come with some of the highest fees and commissions, which largely fund the guarantees they offer. A practical indicator of a well-designed policy that truly benefits you is if your accumulated cash value at the five or six-year mark at least equals, or even surpasses, your total premiums paid. As always, you should pay close attention to the fine print and approach an overly optimistic sales pitch with healthy skepticism.

3. **Variable Life Insurance**

   VL's are frequently marketed as investment-friendly policies. They are similar to Universal Life but with more flexibility, and annually determined rates, costs, and fees. VL's allow you to allocate premiums to sub-accounts that mimic mutual funds. However, the investment risk falls entirely on you, and the associated fees can eat away at returns.
4. **Premium Financing Arrangements**

   These involve borrowing money to pay premiums on high-value policies, with the promise of significant financial benefits. In reality, these arrangements are often complex, risky, and unsuitable for many consumers.

Remember, working with a fiduciary can make all the difference in figuring out what plan type is best for your individual needs and situation.

How to Protect Yourself

- **Ask for Simplicity**: The best policies can be explained clearly. If an agent can't explain a product and cannot offer clear examples so that you understand, it's time to dig deeper.
- **Read the Fine Print**: Complex products often come with many fees and charges, conditions, or terms, that reduce or limit the actual cash value.
- **Consult an Expert**: LIR specializes in breaking down these products to ensure you understand them clearly.

Give yourself the confidence of fully understanding your options and making sure that the policy you choose is one that you fully comprehend.

A Temptation to Avoid: Online Quotes

Online life insurance quotes may seem like a convenient way to compare policies, but they rarely provide the full picture. These quotes are designed to attract your attention with low rates, often excluding critical details like fees, exclusions, and actual eligibility criteria.

The problem with online quotes is that they give a false sense of simplicity. They're designed to get you in the door, but once you start the application process, the numbers often change dramatically.

What Online Quotes Don't Show You

1. **Health and Lifestyle Adjustments**
   Many online tools assume ideal health conditions, which rarely apply to real-world applicants. Once your health history and lifestyle factors are considered, the quoted premiums often increase.
2. **Policy Exclusions**
   Online quotes typically don't disclose policy exclusions, such as high-risk hobbies or specific medical conditions.
3. **Limited Options - Despite Their Claim**
   There are many excellent insurance companies that don't partner with marketing firms or online quoting platforms, and therefore won't appear in your search results. These "hidden gem" insurers often have high ratings (A+), and can deliver superior coverage for less money because they avoid considerable costs from marketing and advertising campaigns.

How to Protect Yourself

Many online quoting companies are also lead generators. Their purpose is to find a person looking for life insurance and either sell them a generic product, with no consideration for their specific needs, or to get them into the sales pipeline to upsell them on higher-cost products. So make sure to:

- **Avoid Making Decisions Based on Price Alone**: The cheapest option isn't always the best fit. Consider the policy's terms, coverage, and potential hidden costs.
- **Use Online Tools as a Starting Point**: Treat online quotes as a rough estimate and dig deeper into the details before committing.

Advice vs. Information: The Critical Difference

One of the biggest red flags to watch out for is an agent or broker who provides advice rather than information. While this may seem helpful on the surface, advice often reflects their sales objectives rather than your best interest.

Advice is inherently biased—it's tailored to align with what the agent wants you to do. True empowerment comes from receiving information that allows you to make your own decisions.

Signs You're Receiving Advice Instead of Information

1. **Limited Options**

   If an agent presents only one or two policies, they may be steering you toward products that benefit them rather than you.

2. **Sales-Driven Language**
   Phrases like "This is perfect for you" or "This is the best option on the market" signal a lack of impartiality.
3. **Lack of Transparency**
   An agent offering advice may gloss over important details, such as exclusions, fees, or limitations, to make the policy appear more attractive.

How to Protect Yourself

- **Request a Comprehensive Overview**: Ask for a breakdown of all available options, including their pros and cons.
- **Verify the Details**: Use resources like LifeInsuranceReview.com to ensure the policy aligns with your needs.
- **Focus on Empowerment**: Choose an advisor who prioritizes education over making the sale.

Life insurance is too important to rely solely on the advice of someone who has skin in the game. Information, however, is impartial and can be used to make a decision that is best for your needs.

Recognizing Red Flags: A Quick Checklist

To safeguard yourself during the life insurance buying process, watch out for these red flags:

- ☐ Pressure-based tactics designed to rush your decision.
- ☐ Policies with promises that seem too good to be true.
- ☐ General descriptions of great benefits and features that lack clear details
- ☐ Advice that feels sales-driven rather than impartial.

By staying vigilant and informed, you can avoid the pitfalls of being sold a policy that doesn't serve your best interests.

When it comes to life insurance, empowerment is key. The ultimate goal isn't just to purchase a policy but to know that the decision reflects your unique needs and priorities. Unfortunately, many agents approach the process from a perspective of convincing rather than informing. This approach leaves consumers feeling uncertain or pressured, rather than confident and empowered. It is important to understand your options, and know which one is most appropriate for you, rather than relying solely on what a salesperson told you.

As my partner James emphasizes, "You know your life better than anyone else—you need resources to help you explore, compare, and verify, not someone telling you what to believe."

Don't Trust Blind Conviction—Trust Yourself

Agents or brokers who rely heavily on persuasive tactics often steer clients toward decisions that reflect their own biases, rather than the client's best interests. They may come across as confident or authoritative, but confidence doesn't equal accuracy. This is why it's essential to trust yourself and prioritize your understanding of your needs over an agent's sales pitch.

Why Convincing Is Problematic

We have talked about this in previous chapters, but it bears repeating. The agent or broker who is trying to convince you is often engaging in the "magic show." This is the opposite of empowering you. Why would they do this? To conceal these glaring red flags:

1. **Bias in Product Recommendations**
   Agents and brokers tied to specific insurance companies often have a limited portfolio of products to sell. Their recommendations are often shaped by these limitations, even if better options exist elsewhere.
2. **Conflict of Interest**
   Salespeople earn commissions on sales, and the size of these commissions varies depending on the product. Policies with higher premiums or more complex structures often result in bigger commissions for agents, which can influence their recommendations.
3. **The "Hard Sell" Approach**
   Agents may try to overwhelm you with details, figures, or jargon, in an attempt to push you toward agreeing with their perspective. This isn't empowerment—it's manipulation.

The Empowerment Approach

The best insurance decisions come from understanding your own needs and taking the time to compare your options. An empowered consumer asks questions, seeks clarity, and ultimately makes choices based on facts—not persuasion.

Interview Your Agent: What You Need to Know

My mother used to tell me: Choose your friends, don't let them choose you. I now add a corollary to this rule: Choose your life insurance policy, don't let your friend choose it for you. Don't let your friend's affiliation with an insurance company choose the future protection of your family.

Just because your good friend now works for XYZ Insurance, it does not mean that XYZ Insurance has the product that is right for you.

The agent or broker you choose will have a direct impact on the quality of the policy you end up with, so it's essential to ensure they're qualified and aligned with your needs.

Questions to Ask During the Interview

1. **How Long Have You Been an Active Agent or Broker?**
   Experience matters. Look for those who have at least five years of full working experience (not just the age of their license), as they are more likely to have a broader understanding of the market and the nuances of different policies.
2. **Are You a Captive Agent or an Independent Agent?**
   Captive agents work for a single insurance company and can only sell that company's products, while independent agents have access to policies from multiple insurers. Understanding this distinction can help you gauge whether you're getting a full range of options.
3. **Does your license require you to be a fiduciary for your customers/clients?**
   Life insurance sales professionals are not fiduciaries, meaning they may not be legally obligated to prioritize your best interests. A fiduciary-focused advisor is more likely to provide unbiased guidance. LIR is proud to represent the highest level of fiduciary in the industry, which is a Licensed Life Insurance Analyst. Less than 1% of life insurance professionals have this designation.

4. **Can You Explain This Policy in Plain Language?**
   If an agent struggles to explain the key features of a policy in a way you can understand, it may indicate that they're relying on selling points rather than substance.
5. **What Is Your Approach to Reviews and Updates?**
   Policies need to evolve as your life changes. Ask how often the agent conducts reviews and whether they provide ongoing support after the sale.

When to Walk Away

During your conversations with an agent, be on the lookout for warning signs that they may not have your best interests at heart.

1. **Avoidance of Specific Questions**
   If an agent dodges questions or provides vague answers, it's a major red flag. Clear communication is essential in helping you make an informed decision.
2. **Pressure to Act Quickly**
   An agent who insists on immediate action without giving you time to consider your options may be more interested in their commission than your needs.
3. **Overemphasis on a Limited Amount of Products and Insurance Companies**
   Be wary of agents who focus exclusively on one type of policy or one insurance provider. This often indicates a lack of flexibility or an underlying bias.

4. **Lack of Transparency About Fees and Compensation**
   Agents or brokers should be upfront about how they're compensated and whether it may impact the advice they provide.

LIR's Checklist for Vetting an Agent or Broker

At LIR, we believe that consumers deserve transparency and respect throughout the insurance process. To that end, we've developed a checklist to help you evaluate potential agents and ensure they're a good fit for your needs.

The LIR Checklist

- ✓ **Years of Experience:** At least five years of full-time work experience is ideal to ensure the agent has a track record and sufficient expertise.
- ✓ **Access to Multiple Providers**: Independent agents typically offer a wider range of options than captive agents.
- ✓ **Fiduciary Commitment**: Verify whether the agent or broker is legally obligated to prioritize your interests. Licensed Life Insurance Analyst is the highest level of fiduciary in the industry. LIR maintains this designation.
- ✓ **Willingness to Answer Questions**: The agent should be comfortable addressing your concerns and explaining policies in detail.
- ✓ **Post-Sale Support**: Ask whether they offer periodic reviews and ongoing assistance to adjust your policy as needed.

Don't forget that you have built-in protection, by way of the free look period. This is your final opportunity to review your policy with a fiduciary to make sure that your interests are protected and that you understand exactly what you are buying (or were sold!).

The Consequences of Poor Advice

Failing to thoroughly vet your agent or broker and policy can lead to significant and far-reaching consequences. One of the most critical risks is inadequate coverage. Without proper guidance, you may find yourself with a policy that doesn't align with your actual needs, leaving your family exposed and financially vulnerable in the event of your passing. A death benefit that falls short of covering essential expenses can devastate your loved ones during an already challenging time.

Another common issue is the burden of excessive costs. Some agents and brokers, motivated by hitting their sale goals, might steer you toward policies with unnecessary features or inflated premiums. This approach can result in you overpaying for coverage that doesn't offer proportional value, draining your resources and hindering your financial goals.

Equally concerning is the confusion that arises from poorly explained policies. Complex products, often loaded with jargon and technical terms, can be difficult to understand without clear and transparent communication. When sold without proper explanation, these policies leave you uncertain about what you're paying for or whether your coverage is adequate. This lack of clarity can undermine the peace of mind life insurance is meant to provide, making it all the more important to carefully evaluate your life insurance sales professional's expertise and commitment to your needs.

How LIR Turns Red Flags to Green

At LIR, our mission is to empower consumers by providing the tools and knowledge needed to make informed decisions. Unlike traditional agents, we focus on education rather than sales, helping you explore, compare, and verify policies to find the best fit for your needs.

The LIR Process

1. **Independent Reviews**
   We evaluate policies without bias, ensuring that you understand every aspect of your coverage.
2. **Tailored Recommendations**
   By thoroughly assessing your financial goals and personal circumstances, we help you identify the policy that offers the greatest value and best fits your needs.
3. **Ongoing Support**
   LIR offers periodic reviews to ensure your policy evolves with your life, providing peace of mind for years to come.

Conclusion: Empowerment Over Persuasion

The best insurance decisions are made when you're empowered to explore, compare, and verify. By taking the time to interview your agent, ask the right questions, and watch for red flags, you can ensure that your policy reflects your unique goals and priorities. With resources like LIR, you'll never have to rely on blind trust, you'll have the knowledge and support needed to make decisions with confidence.

CHAPTER TWELVE

HOW LIFEINSURANCEREVIEW.COM (LIR) CAN HELP PROTECT YOUR FAMILY'S FUTURE

Benefit from our specialized expertise! Whether you're exploring life insurance options, comparing plans, or reviewing your current policy, we're here to provide the clarity you need. It's time to go from believing to knowing.

– lifeinsurancereview.com

LIR did not happen by accident. My partners, team, and I have all experienced the frustrations and obfuscations of the life insurance industry. Our goal was to create a platform where people get unbiased information to make well informed decisions about life insurance policies.

We created LIR so you would be empowered, not sold.

So you know, not just believe.

When it comes to life insurance, it's an essential asset for your financial planning foundation. Your family's financial future depends on having the right policy in place, a policy that aligns with your unique needs, goals, and circumstances. I want to expose the traditional life insurance sales process, riddled with conflicts of interest and misinformation, that often makes it difficult to achieve this goal. I want you to be empowered to make informed, confident decisions about your life insurance coverage.

Our proof of concept? About 90% of the life insurance policies we review can be improved upon.

We created LIR because we saw a clear need: the life insurance sales industry often prioritizes pushing products over truly serving your best interests.

Help to Navigate the Life Insurance Landscape

The life insurance industry is designed to sell, not to serve. Agents and brokers are often incentivized by commissions, hitting sales goals, and other perks to prioritize policies that benefit their bottom line rather than your best interests. This sales-driven model can leave consumers with policies that are overpriced, mismatched to their needs, or unnecessarily complex.

LIR operates as a counterbalance to this system. Our fiduciary independent reviews are designed to protect you from the pitfalls of the life insurance sales process. Unlike traditional agents or brokers working with marketing companies, we are not beholden to any insurance company or product. Our sole obligation is to you, the client. By providing unbiased, comprehensive reviews, we ensure that the policy you choose serves your best interests, not someone else's.

As my partner James puts it, "Most consumers think their agent has their back, but the reality is that many agents are tied to a sales quota or a limited portfolio of products. At LIR, we break through that conflict to help you find the coverage you actually need."

What LIR Does and How You Benefit

LIR is a consumer-first resource designed to demystify the life insurance process and help you make the best possible decision. We are consumer advocates focusing on education, transparency, and empowerment.

Our Approach

1. **Unbiased Guidance**
   As fiduciaries, our team is legally obligated to act in your best interest. This means you can trust that the guidance and insights we provide are free from conflicts of interest or hidden agendas.
2. **Comprehensive Reviews**
   Every policy we evaluate undergoes a rigorous 28-point review process, which examines everything from coverage adequacy and exclusions to fees and policy performance.
3. **Educational Empowerment**
   We believe that informed consumers make better decisions. That's why we provide clear, actionable information about your policy options, helping you explore, compare, and verify before making a commitment.

The Benefits of Working with LIR

- **Clarity**: Gain a clear understanding of what your policy does and doesn't cover, as well as how it aligns with your goals.

- **Confidence**: Make decisions with confidence, knowing that you've explored all your options and chosen the best fit.
- **Savings**: Avoid poorly designed life insurance policies that have high expenses and charges.
- **Protection**: Ensure your financial security with a policy that delivers on its promises.

The 28-Point Review Process: Ensuring Your Policy is Right for You

One of the cornerstones of LIR's approach is our proprietary 28-point review process. This comprehensive evaluation is designed to uncover hidden pitfalls, highlight opportunities for improvement, and ensure that your policy provides maximum value.

What the 28-Point Review Covers

- **Coverage Adequacy**: Does the policy's death benefit align with your financial obligations and goals?
- **Exclusions**: Are there conditions that could prevent your policy from paying out when it's needed most?
- **Policy Structure:** Is the policy optimally designed for maximum benefits?
- **Fees and Costs**: Are there hidden costs or rising premiums that could erode the value of your policy?
- **Policy Riders**: Are the additional features you're paying for still necessary or relevant?
- **Policy Performance**: For cash value policies, is the growth rate meeting expectations?

- **Comparative Analysis to other available options:** how do we know what we have is good if we don't have clear and thorough comparison options?
- **Financial, tax, and estate planning considerations:** to make sure it serves and fits your own goals and planning.

Our 28-point review isn't just about catching mistakes, it's about ensuring that your policy works 100% for you, not against you. By the end of the process, you'll have a clear understanding of what you're paying for and why.

Explore, Compare, Verify: The LIR Philosophy

At LifeInsuranceReview.com, we operate under a simple but powerful philosophy: Explore, Compare, and Verify.

- **Explore**: We encourage clients to explore their options thoroughly, considering all types of policies and providers. This ensures you don't settle for the first policy presented to you, which might not be the best fit.
- **Compare**: By comparing multiple policies side by side, we help you identify the one that offers the best combination of coverage, cost, and value.
- **Verify**: Our fiduciary reviews serve as your last line of defense, verifying that the policy you choose aligns with your goals and is free from hidden pitfalls.

This approach shifts the power dynamic, putting you, not the agent or insurance company, in control of the decision-making process.

The Certifications Behind the LIR Team

You won't find top sales awards or memorabilia documenting sales achievements on our desks. But you will find designations on our walls. We believe that expertise matters, especially when you're navigating something as complex and consequential as life insurance. That's why the team at LIR is composed of highly credentialed professionals with extensive experience in insurance, financial planning, and legal analysis.

Key Certifications

- **CLU® (Chartered Life Underwriter)**: This designation represents the highest level of expertise in life insurance, with a focus on advanced client servicing and policy design.
- **ChFC® (Chartered Financial Consultant)**: Specialists in comprehensive financial planning, with an emphasis on integrating life insurance into broader strategies.
- **CFP® (Certified Financial Planner)**: Known as the gold standard in financial planning, bring a comprehensive and holistic approach to the life insurance review process.
- **CPA & EA (Enrolled Agent)**: Tax experts who provide insights into the tax implications of life insurance policies. CPAs are also skilled in analyzing policy performance calculations and conducting stress testing.
- **FINRA Licenses (e.g., Series 6, 7, 63, 65):** Necessary for evaluating policies with investment components, such as variable life insurance, variable annuities, and registered index-linked annuities.

- **We are licensed life insurance professionals** (License Type: Life Insurance, Variable Life, and Life Settlement), and can practice in all 50 states, the District of Columbia, and three U.S. territories. NIPR serves as a licensing and compliance resource for insurance professionals, offering expertise, agile technical solutions, innovative tools, and data to support the evolving needs of state regulators and the insurance industry.

Since 2011, our life insurance agency has completed thousands of in-depth life insurance reviews, building a strong reputation for expertise and trust. Recently, we earned the prestigious distinction of being licensed as life insurance analyst professionals by the California Department of Insurance—a credential held by fewer than 1% of life insurance professionals. An even smaller percentage of agencies hold this license at the entity level, as we do, further elevating our standing in the industry.

Under the current leadership of attorney James G. Burns, JD, LL.M, TEP®, SBC #208656, who has been in practice since 2000, our TEAM possesses a deep understanding of the complexities inherent in life insurance products. We recognize that life insurance policies are fundamentally legal contracts and expertly review all types of life insurance options to craft comprehensive and effective estate and financial planning strategies. Our meticulous life insurance review process ensures that our recommendations are both thorough and well-rounded.

CPA professionals are indispensable to the structural integrity of our Leadership TEAM. Our in-house accounting and tax authorities are not only adept in life insurance but also excel in tax and financial planning. Our comprehensive review services extend to include insightful tax planning and cash value performance analysis. CPAs hold the highest trust among consumers due to their well-earned reputation for accounting and tax expertise.

Our firm is adept at managing life insurance tax cases across all 50 states, underscoring the importance of having Enrolled Agents (EAs) on our Leadership TEAM. Our member professionals are not only experienced in life insurance but also hold the highest credential awarded by the IRS for tax expertise. Their dual proficiency in tax and life insurance matters is crucial for providing our life insurance review cases with holistic financial solutions.

The LIR TEAM has membership in the following associations:

- **Society of Trust and Estate Practitioners (STEP)** – founded by George Tasker in 1991 and is the international professional body for advisers who specialize in inheritance and succession planning. Its members are mostly attorneys, accountants, tax advisers, trust officers and trust administrators as well as banking and insurance professionals in the trust field.
- **Financial Planning Association (FPA)** – the largest membership organization in the US that represents financial planners. The organization was formed from the merger of the Institute of Certified Financial Planners and the International Association for Financial Planning. The International Association for Financial Planning was founded in 1970 and the Institute of Certified

Financial Planners was formed in 1973 by the first graduating class of the College for Financial Planning.

- **The American Institute of Certified Public Accountants (AICPA)** – the national professional organization of Certified Public Accountants (CPAs) in the United States, with more than 428,000 members in 130 countries. Founded in 1887 as the American Association of Public Accountants (AAPA), the organization sets ethical standards and U.S. auditing standards.
- **The California Society of Certified Public Accountants (CalCPA)** – founded in 1909, and is the largest statewide professional association of certified public accountants in the United States with more than 42,000 members. Affiliated with CalCPA, the CalCPA Education Foundation focuses on continuous professional development, providing a variety of educational programs and resources to enhance the skills and knowledge of accounting professionals.

James highlights the importance of these credentials: "When you work with LIR, you're not just getting a review, you're getting the collective expertise of a team that understands every nuance of the life insurance landscape."

Why Fiduciaries Are Key to Protecting Your Interests

The fiduciary standard is what sets LIR apart from traditional agents and brokers. Unlike sales-driven advisors, fiduciaries are legally obligated to prioritize your best interests. This means no hidden agendas, no conflicts of interest, and no pressure to buy products that don't align with your goals.

By working with a fiduciary, you gain an advocate who is solely focused on helping you achieve financial security for your family. This level of trust and transparency is essential in an industry where misinformation and conflicts of interest are all too common.

How LIR Protects Your Family's Future

At the end of the day, the mission of LIR is simple: to protect you and your family from being misled or underserved in the life insurance market. By offering independent, fiduciary-focused reviews, we help clients navigate the complexities of life insurance with confidence and clarity.

A policy isn't just paperwork; it's a safety net for your family's future. LIR developed specialized services to guide clients at every stage of their life insurance journey. Whether reviewing an existing policy, comparing options before purchase, or leveraging the free look period, LIR ensures that your coverage aligns perfectly with your needs and goals.

Reviewing Existing Policies: Fixing What's Broken

Too often, clients come to LIR after discovering their policies don't meet their expectations. Maybe the coverage amount is insufficient, the premiums are unsustainable, or the fine print reveals limitations they hadn't anticipated.

We've even reviewed Indexed Universal Life (IUL) policies just about five years after issue and found that the actual cash value performance was worse than even the originally illustrated worst-case scenario, falling short of the optimistic projections clients were sold on. What's more concerning is when this underperformance occurred during a period of strong market growth post 2009, in the S&P 500 index. Through a detailed, independent review of the in-force illustration, we help clients identify these shortfalls early and provide actionable strategies to correct course or explore better policy alternatives.

LIR's 28-point review process scrutinizes every detail, from coverage adequacy to policy performance. This review process is not just about identifying flaws—it's about providing solutions. If a policy isn't working for you, LIR ensures that you have the knowledge and tools to make an informed change, whether it's optimizing, upgrading, converting, or replacing the policy altogether.

Don't Know Where to Start?

If you are wondering the best way to approach the life insurance process, we have some guidance. This decision guide provides a clear process that empowers you to make the best choices. Given the abundance of information and options available, our methodical review approach ensures thoroughness, critical analysis, and effectiveness in assisting you throughout the decision-making process.

Knowledge & Experience

What are your expectations, budget, requirements, and goals when it comes to securing a policy? The primary purpose behind your need for life insurance should be crystal clear, whether it's to protect your family, cover a mortgage, or support your business. Without this clarity, you risk being sold a policy that doesn't match your needs.

Health & Medical History

Are you aware of your current health status and any areas that might impact your policy? Do you fully understand your medical history, including conditions that could affect underwriting? Surprises during the application process—such as an unexpected health rating—can lead to higher premiums or even declined coverage. Be proactive: assess your health, make improvements where possible, and work closely with your financial professional, agent, or broker to strategize for the best possible outcome.

Research & Comparisons

Have you taken the time to research and compare policies from multiple insurers? Don't rely solely on one agent or broker's assurance that they've found the "best option." Request multiple quotes, compare illustrations, and dive into the details to understand what each policy offers.

Resources & More...

At the end of this book, following the 12 case studies, you'll find additional resources, such as this helpful decision guide framework.

The LIR Decision Guide with Questions:

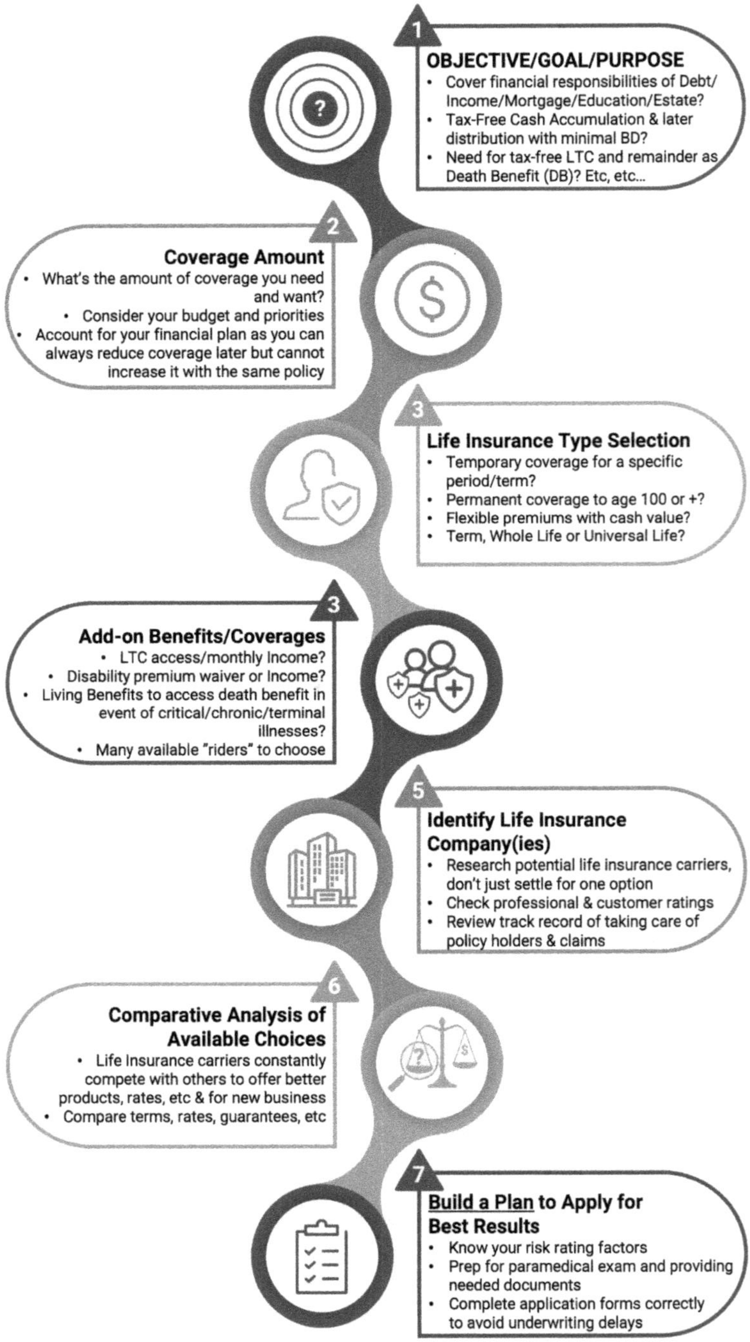

Comparing Policies Before Purchase: Making Informed Decisions

Buying a life insurance policy is one of the most important financial decisions you'll make. Yet many people rush into it without fully understanding their options. LIR acts as your safeguard, ensuring that you enter this commitment with your eyes wide open.

LIR's fiduciary advisors work with you to compare multiple policies side by side. This involves breaking down complex terms into clear, understandable information. We analyze key factors such as:

- **Premium Costs**: Are the premiums affordable and sustainable over the long term?
- **Coverage Adequacy**: Does the policy provide enough coverage to meet your family's financial needs?
- **Policy Features**: Are additional riders or benefits worth the added cost?
- **Provider Reputation**: What is the insurer's Comdex rating and claims payout history?

By presenting this information in a transparent and unbiased manner, LIR empowers you to make a choice that reflects your goals—not the salesperson's commission structure.

Make the Free Look Period Work for You

The free look period is your last opportunity to ensure your policy is the right fit before committing long-term. Unfortunately, many consumers don't even know this feature exists, and agents are often reluctant to emphasize it. LIR fills this gap, offering an independent review during the free look period to verify that the policy meets your expectations. You will get:

1. **Policy Validation**: LIR ensures that the terms and conditions match what was promised during the sales process.
2. **Benefit Verification**: The death benefit and additional features are evaluated to confirm their alignment with your needs.
3. **Cost Analysis**: Annual policy expenses, Internal Rate of Return (IRR) calculations, and any policy pitfalls are identified and explained.

If discrepancies are found (and they frequently are), LIR provides actionable recommendations for addressing them, whether that means renegotiating the policy, selecting an alternative, or canceling completely.

Partnering with Professionals

LIR doesn't just work directly with consumers; it also partners with trusted professionals to extend its mission of providing independent life insurance counsel. CPAs, estate planning attorneys, realtors, and financial planners/advisors often serve as the first point of contact for clients navigating major life events, such as buying a home, planning for retirement, or taking on an investment or business opportunity.

By collaborating with these professionals, LIR ensures that their clients receive the same unbiased, fiduciary-focused guidance that sets LIR apart. For instance:

- **CPAs**: Clients often turn to CPAs for tax planning, especially when managing estates or businesses. LIR helps these clients evaluate policies for tax efficiency, ensuring that their coverage aligns with broader financial goals.
- **Estate Planning Attorneys:** Clients rely on estate planning attorneys to structure their estates and set up trusts that protect and transfer wealth efficiently. LIR complements this work by providing specialized life insurance planning services, including in-depth policy reviews, to ensure clients have the most suitable and competitive coverage aligned with their estate planning goals.
- **Realtors**: Purchasing a home is one of the most common justifications for buying life insurance. By partnering with LIR, realtors can connect their clients with experts who ensure the policy protects the mortgage and other financial responsibilities without overpaying for unnecessary features.
- **Financial Planners/Advisors**: Life insurance is often a key component of a comprehensive financial plan. LIR supports financial planners, investment advisors and fee-based financial advisors by providing independent, detailed reviews of existing and proposed policies, ensuring that recommendations truly align with the client's best interests and long-term goals.

The 5-Star Standard: LIR's Commitment to Excellence

LIR's goal is simple: to deliver a consistently exceptional experience for every client. We want every experience working with us to be 5 stars. To achieve this, the team adheres to a five-point plan that ensures every client feels respected, informed, and empowered.

1. Respecting You

We honor your values and goals. Our approach is always aligned with your best interest, ensuring you feel heard, respected, and supported.

2. Providing Clear Answers

Your needs and preferences come first. We answer your questions with clarity and professionalism, so you always know where you stand.

3. Being a Trusted Resource

As experienced experts, we are committed to educating, guiding, and delivering meaningful insights that empower and inform.

4. Compare and Verify with Confidence

We walk you through a thoughtful discovery and evaluation process, helping you compare options and verify information so you can make well-informed decisions.

5. Supporting Confident Life Insurance Decisions

Our mission is to equip you with the knowledge, clarity, and tools you need to make life insurance decisions that serve your future with confidence.

The LIR Difference - We Are Consumer Advocates

Unlike traditional agents, LIR puts the client first at every step. Whether you're reviewing, comparing, or verifying a policy, LIR ensures that the process is clear, empowering, and free from conflicts of interest. With a team of credentialed experts and a commitment to fiduciary principles, LIR is setting a new standard for what life insurance guidance should be.

When it comes to life insurance, LIR stands on your side, not the life insurance sales industry. We are guided by core values that place the needs and interests of consumers above all else. These values form the foundation of everything we do, setting us apart from anyone else!

Core Values That Define LIR

1. Client-Centered Transparency

Transparency is at the core of LIR's philosophy. In a market where fine print, complex terms, and sales driven advice are the norm, LIR is committed to providing clear, unbiased, straightforward information. This transparency empowers clients to make informed decisions without fear of being misled or overwhelmed.

Unlike many agents and brokers who obscure policy details to close a sale, LIR ensures that you understand and have clarity with everything. Whether it's a fee structure, illustrations, or benefits, nothing is left to chance.

2. Fiduciary Responsibility

The fiduciary standard is what truly differentiates LIR from traditional life insurance professionals. LIR's advisors are legally obligated to act in your best interest, eliminating conflicts of interest that plague the sales-driven insurance industry. This means no hidden agendas, no upselling, and no compromises, just honest, unbiased counsel tailored to your needs.

Our fiduciary responsibility isn't just a legal obligation, it's a moral one. We believe that everyone deserves life insurance guidance they can trust, free from the motivation of commission-based sales.

3. Empowerment Through Education

LIR believes that an empowered client is an informed client. Education is woven into every step of the process, ensuring that you understand not only what your policy does but also why it's the best fit for your needs.

From decoding policy illustrations to comparing multiple coverage options, LIR's goal is to make the life insurance process as accessible and straightforward as possible. By prioritizing education, we help you take control of your financial future.

4. Respect for Individual Goals

At LIR, there's no one-size-fits-all approach. Every client's situation is unique, and our team takes the time to understand your specific goals, concerns, and financial priorities. Whether you're securing coverage for your growing family, protecting your business, or planning your estate, LIR tailors its guidance to meet your needs, not the needs of a life insurance sales professional's sales goal.

A New Standard in Life Insurance Guidance

Traditional life insurance sales professionals and the life insurance marketing companies often operate with a singular focus: to sell. This approach can leave consumers feeling pressured, confused, and ultimately underserved. In contrast, LIR operates as an advocate for the client, flipping the script on the traditional sales process.

- **Independent Reviews**: LIR is not tied to any insurance company, marketing organization, or product, ensuring that the guidance you receive is unbiased and comprehensive.

- **Focus on Long-Term Relationships**: Unlike agents who move on to the next sale, LIR provides ongoing support, conducting periodic reviews to ensure your policy continues to meet your needs.
- **Comprehensive Expertise**: With a team of credentialed professionals, including CLUs, CFPs, and CPAs, LIR brings a level of expertise rarely found in the industry.
- **Client Empowerment**: LIR's process is designed to put you in the driver's seat, giving you the tools and knowledge to make decisions with confidence.

The difference is simple: we're not here to sell you something. We're here to help you protect your family's future, and that means putting your goals first, every single time.

How to Get Started with LIR

Whether you're reviewing an existing policy or choosing a new one, LIR offers a seamless process designed to meet you where you are. Here's how to take the first step:

1. Compare Policies Before Purchase

If you're in the market for a new policy, LIR can help you navigate the overwhelming number of options. Through a transparent, side-by-side comparison, you'll gain a clear understanding of which policies offer the best combination of cost, coverage, and benefits.

This process includes:

- Breaking down policy features into plain language.
- Evaluating premiums and internal rates of return.

- Assessing the Insurance Company's Comdex score and specific policy history.

LIR's fiduciary advisors provide unbiased recommendations, helping you avoid the pitfalls of pressure-based sales pitches and misleading information.

2. Leverage the Free Look Period (10-30 Days)

For those who have recently purchased a policy, the free look period is a crucial final opportunity to confirm that it's truly the right fit. LIR offers an independent, objective review during this window to verify all policy details, ensuring the coverage aligns with your expectations, meets your needs, and delivers on what was promised.

3. Review Your Existing Policy

If you already have life insurance, the first step is to evaluate whether it still aligns with your goals. LIR's 28-point review process provides a detailed analysis of your policy, highlighting areas where it may fall short and offering actionable recommendations for improvement.

Common issues uncovered during reviews include:

- Insufficient coverage amounts
- High policy charges and expenses
- Design and structuring problems
- Concerns with policy benefits and features

By addressing these issues, LIR ensures that your policy delivers the value and protection your family deserves.

Realizing the Vision: 5-Star Service and Commitment

LIR's standard of excellence is reflected in our 5-star service commitment. This ambitious standard is driven by the belief that every client deserves an exceptional experience. Through respect, transparency, and empowerment, LIR ensures that when you work with us, you feel confident and secure—empowered, never sold.

As our client Juan shares, "I got recruited into a network marketing financial company through my tax accountant, and soon I was pressured to buy a cash value policy because it can grow my money tax free and protect my family at the same time. But after getting my policy reviewed, I learned a lot more than what I was told. I didn't understand the fees, charges, and internal rate of return (IRR) figures. Because of my lack of knowledge, I was taken advantage of, but luckily, I was still able to cancel the policy within the free look period!"

Your Life Insurance Journey Starts Here

Life insurance is one of the most important investments you'll make, and it's too critical to leave to chance. With LIR, you gain a trusted advocate partner who prioritizes your needs, respects you, and empowers you to make informed decisions.

Whether you're comparing new options, leveraging the free look period, or reviewing an existing policy, LIR's comprehensive approach ensures that your coverage provides the protection your family deserves. The process is simple. Go to lifeinsureancereview.com and schedule your free consultation. From there we will ask you questions and discover your life insurance needs. Finally, we will present you with a detailed evaluation, analysis, and options.

You will be empowered to explore, compare, and verify your options and solutions from a life insurance expert that is on your side.

The LifeInsuranceReview.com (LIR) Difference

	LIFE INSURANCE REVIEW	Life Insurance AGENTS[1]	Life Insurance BROKERS[1]	Financial ADVISORS[2]	Other Financial PROFESSIONALS (Attorney, CPA, CFP®, etc)
Life Insurance Analyst Licensed	✓	✗	✗	✗	✗
Life Insurance Licensed	✓	✓	✓	✓	?
Sales Focus	Review Focus	✓	✓	Mostly ✓	?
Work on Commissions	Fee-Based	✓	✓	Mostly ✓	?
Have Financial Incentives for Sales Productions: Promotions, Bonuses, Trips, Prizes, etc.	No Sales Incentives	✓	✓	Mostly ✓	?
Fiduciary "...must act in your best interest."	✓	✗	✗	Mostly ✗	Mostly ✓
Charge a Fee for Service	✓	✗	✗	Mostly ✗	Mostly ✓
Life Insurance Products (Term, Whole Life, UL, IUL, GUL, VUL), Annuities, Disability, and LTC	Full	Limited w/ Restrictions	More w/ Limits[3]	Limited[3]	Limited[3]
Life Insurance Company Offerings of 25+	Full	Limited w/ Restrictions	More w/ Limits[3]	Limited[3]	Limited[3]
Variable Life Insurance Options (latest guarantees & flexibilities)	✓	Mostly ✗	Mostly ✗	If FINRA Registered	Mostly ✗
Exclusively Dedicated to Life Insurance Review Services[4]	✓	✗	✗	✗	✗
10+ Years of Life Insurance Review Services	✓	?	?	?	?
Proven TEAM Approach to Independent Life Insurance Reviews	✓	✗	✗	✗	✗
Proven Expertise in Tax Planning	✓	✗	✗	?	?
Proven Expertise in Estate Planning	✓	✗	✗	?	?
Proven Expertise in Financial Planning	✓	✗	✗	?	?
Proven Expertise in Investment Planning	✓	✗	✗	?	?
Expert Background in Accounting, Finance & Business as it Relates to Life Insurance Planning	✓	✗	✗	?	?

1. *Sells also annuities, health insurance, disability, long-term care, final expense, and/or other life insurance products with investment options if associated with a Broker Dealer and FINRA Registered.*
2. *The term "financial advisor" is broad, covering professionals from insurance sales to investment management. This allows insurance agents and brokers to also present themselves as financial advisors, but they mainly push life insurance products and annuities.*
3. *Still limited because most work through a marketing organization for contracting and don't qualify for or have access to life insurance companies with direct contracts only.*
4. *Review services include analysis, comparisons, planning options, and tailored recommendations.*

CONCLUSION

EMPOWERMENT THROUGH KNOWLEDGE

"The best time to plant a tree was 20 years ago. The second-best time is now." (The same goes for life insurance.)

— **Chinese Proverb** (adapted)

I've laid out the facts, shared real-life case studies, and given you the insights most people never hear about when it comes to life insurance. You now have the knowledge to level the playing field—to make informed, responsible decisions, and to take full ownership of your life insurance planning.

You also know what to ask, who to ask, and where to turn when you need a second opinion or a professional review of your policy. This is the kind of information the life insurance sales industry doesn't openly share. But now, you have it.

So, where do you go from here?

You move forward empowered. You understand the landscape, the players, the products, and your choices. Whether you decide to purchase life insurance online or through a professional, you now know that **LifeInsuranceReview.com (LIR)** exists for one reason: to be the consumer advocate and champion.

We are not here to sell to you. We are here to protect your interests, ensure you are never misled, never limited in your options, and never sold short.

From this point on, you can move forward with confidence because now, **you know better.**

The Core Takeaways

1. The Importance of Fiduciary Guidance

We began this journey by examining the importance of fiduciaries—professionals who are legally obligated to act in your best interest. Unlike traditional agents and brokers who operate within a system rife with conflicts of interest, fiduciaries prioritize your needs over their own commissions or incentives.

LIR embodies this fiduciary principle. Its mission is to serve as a trusted partner, empowering you to explore, compare, and verify policies without bias. Whether you're reviewing an existing policy, purchasing a new one, or using the free look period to evaluate your decision, fiduciary guidance ensures that you are fully informed and in control.

2. Understanding Policy Types and Common Pitfalls

We explored the major types of life insurance products—term, whole, universal, and variable—and their respective benefits and drawbacks. These policies are tools, each with its strengths and weaknesses, and the "best" policy is the one that aligns with your individual goals and financial situation.

We also delved into the hidden costs and pitfalls that can derail consumers. From misleading policy illustrations to exclusions buried in the fine print, the life insurance industry is filled with potential traps. By understanding these dangers, you can protect yourself and ensure your policy delivers on its promises.

3. Life Changes Require Life Insurance Reviews

Life is not static, and neither are your insurance needs. Marriage, children, home ownership, and career changes all impact the coverage you require. Failing to review and update your policy can leave you underinsured or paying for features you no longer need.

Periodic reviews, like those offered by LifeInsuranceReview.com (LIR), ensure that your coverage evolves alongside your life. They provide a safety net, protecting you from outdated policies and uncovering opportunities to optimize your coverage.

4. The Free Look Period: Your Last Line of Defense

One of the most critical tools for consumers is the free look period—a brief window during which you can review and cancel your policy without penalty. This period is your opportunity to step back from the pressure-based sales environment and evaluate whether your policy truly meets your needs.

LIR excels at helping clients use this time effectively. By conducting thorough reviews, we uncover discrepancies, clarify terms, and provide actionable recommendations, ensuring that you're confident in your decision.

5. The Protection of Empowerment

Throughout this book, we've emphasized the difference between being sold and being empowered. When you're sold, you're at the mercy of someone else's agenda. When you're empowered, you have the knowledge and tools to make decisions that reflect your values and priorities.

Empowerment means asking questions, seeking clarity, and taking the time to understand your options. It means choosing policies based on your needs—not someone else's incentives. Most importantly, it means having the confidence to know that you're protecting your family's future in the best way possible.

Reclaiming Control Over the Process

The life insurance sales industry can feel like a one-sided game. Agents, brokers, and financial advisors are often incentivized to sell, not to serve. Consumers are left to navigate a maze of complex products, misleading projections, and pressure-based sales tactics. But it doesn't have to be this way.

LIR was founded to level the playing field. Our mission is deeply personal. We've seen the harm caused by bad policies, the stress of families left unprotected, and the frustration of consumers who feel misled. That's why we created a service designed to protect consumers from these pitfalls and empower them to make informed choices.

By exploring options, comparing policies, and verifying every detail, LIR ensures that you're not just buying a product—you're investing in peace of mind.

Your Next Steps

As you close this book, you're equipped with the knowledge and tools to take control of your life insurance journey. But knowledge is only the first step. Action is what transforms information into security, confidence, and a better future for your family.

Don't Let Your Agent or Broker Determine Your Options - Explore, Compare, and Verify

Their recommendations may be influenced by commissions, sales goal incentives, or limited affiliations with specific companies. Instead, take charge of the process by exploring a wide range of policies, comparing their features and costs, and verifying that they meet your unique needs and goals. With the right information and tools, you can ensure that your decision is informed, unbiased, and truly in your best interest.

Review Your Existing Policy

If you already have a life insurance policy, start by reviewing it in detail. Does it still meet your needs? Are there hidden costs or exclusions you weren't aware of? Use LIR and the 28-point review process to evaluate its effectiveness.

Compare Before You Commit

If you're in the market for a new policy, take the time to explore and compare your options. Don't settle for the first policy presented to you, and don't let sales tactics cloud your judgment. Use the tools and questions provided in this book to ensure that your choice reflects your goals and priorities.

Leverage the Free Look Period (10-30 Days)

If you've recently purchased a policy, the free look period is your opportunity to double-check your decision. Use this time to seek independent advice, clarify terms, and ensure that the policy delivers on its promises.

Final Thoughts

Throughout this book, we've examined the realities of the life insurance sales industry, including its challenges, its pitfalls, and the powerful outcomes available to those who are informed.

As you move forward, remember this: **you are in control.** With the right knowledge, resources, and guidance, you can navigate the life insurance process on your terms. You can protect your loved ones, secure your future, and make choices that align with your individual goals and values—not someone else's agenda.

LifeInsuranceReview.com (LIR) is here to support you every step of the way. Whether you're shopping for a policy, reviewing an existing one, or simply verifying that you're on the right track, our mission is simple: to advocate for you by providing transparent, clear, and unbiased information so you can make the best decisions for yourself, your family, and your future.

🎁 Bonus Gift for Finishing the Book!

As a thank-you for reading to the end, we're giving you access to our **LIR *Don't Be Sold-Empowerment* Kit**—a powerful resource to help you take the next step in your life insurance journey with clarity and confidence.

Plus, use the exclusive code **LIRBOOKFINISH** to receive **50% off** your LifeInsuranceReview.com service fee.

👉 [Download the Don't Be Sold-Empowerment Kit here: *lifeinsurancereview.com/free-look-period*]

Take advantage of this bonus, and let us help you make sure your life insurance truly works for you—not the person who sold it to you.

APPENDIX

12 CASE STUDIES

CASE STUDY 1: Being Sold To – When "Professional Advice" Costs You More for Less

CASE: A young couple in their early 30s had just purchased their first home and were expecting their first child. Like many new parents, they felt a growing sense of responsibility to protect their financial future.

Through a friend's referral, they met with a life insurance agent. **They assumed (like many people do) that working with a licensed insurance professional meant they'd receive advice that puts their interests first.**

Eager to secure protection and check life insurance off their list, they didn't shop around or get a second opinion.

The agent recommended a combination of **two whole life policies** and **two term life policies**, one of each for both the husband and wife. The whole life policies were pitched as "cash value savings tools," while the term coverage was framed as "affordable temporary protection." It all sounded reasonable, so they signed up without fully understanding the structure, costs, or long-term implications.

CHALLENGE: One year later, reality sets in. Between mortgage payments, baby expenses, and everyday living costs, the **monthly premiums for all four policies were stretching their budget thin**.

They started to question:

- Why do we have four policies?
- Do we really need to grow cash value at this stage?
- Are there better savings vehicles?
- Are we overpaying?

That's when they found **LifeInsuranceReview.com (LIR)** and requested a second opinion—something they wished they had done from the beginning.

After the independent review and personalized needs analysis, the uncovered a common issue:

> They had been **sold a product-heavy solution** that prioritized the agent's compensation over the couple's actual needs. Like many life insurance agents and brokers, there are built-in incentives that reward higher policy counts, often leading to recommendations driven more by commission structures than by what's truly in the client's best interest.

Their original intentions—to protect each other and their growing family—were spot on. But the solution they were **sold was overly complex, expensive, and misaligned with their current life stage**. The structure of the policies created **unnecessary financial strain**, while the agent received higher commissions from the whole life portion of the plan.

SOLUTION: The LIR team provided a more suitable, simplified approach:

- One term life insurance policy for each spouse, customized to their needs.
- Each term policy included critical, chronic, and terminal illness riders for extra living benefit protection.
- Each term policy had built-in conversion options, allowing them to switch to permanent coverage later if desired, without needing to re-qualify medically.

This design gave them the **right amount of coverage**, aligned with their goals as young parents and new homeowners, and **cut their total premiums by more than 70%**.

RESULT: This couple fell into a common trap:

- They assumed a professional's recommendation was automatically the right one for them.
- They didn't ask the right questions. They didn't get a second opinion. And they overpaid for coverage they didn't truly need.

After working with the LIR team:

- They now have more appropriate coverage at half the cost.
- They're redirecting the savings into retirement accounts and a college fund for their child.

- Most importantly, they're moving forward with financial confidence, having made a decision based on a protection strategy and planning.

TAKEAWAY: Even licensed insurance professionals can sometimes recommend overly complex and expensive products driven by commission incentives rather than client needs. It's crucial for consumers, especially young families, to seek **independent, fiduciary advice** and get a second opinion before committing to to a specific life insurance product. Simplifying coverage to match true needs not only reduces costs significantly but also builds a stronger, more confident financial foundation for the future. All options should be presented; it is up to the client to decide what best fits their needs.

CASE STUDY 2: Getting the Right Second Opinion – Most Professionals Prioritize Products Over Actual Planning and Putting the Clients First

CASE: A couple, now in their mid-50s, originally sought life insurance to protect each other and two teenage sons in the event of a premature death. Nine years later, their top concern had shifted—not toward leaving an inheritance, but to protecting their retirement savings and investments from potential **long-term care (LTC)** costs.

About nine years ago, they purchased **two whole life policies**, along with **20-year term policies on each of them**, through an insurance broker referred by a friend (with whom they no longer keep in touch).

Roughly a year ago, they were introduced to a new financial advisor, referred by another friend, who held only a FINRA Series 6 and 63 registration but presented himself as a retirement planning expert with a large mutual life insurance company. He recommended replacing both the whole life and term policies with new **"improved" whole life policies** that promised better cash value growth and the same death benefit coverage.

His professional advice: reduce contributions to their 401(k) plans and prioritize funding the new whole life policies instead. The reason? To reduce stock market exposure and shift more into what he claimed was a more tax-efficient and stable long-term investment, backed by the company's 150+ year history of consistent dividends.

Trusting his credentials and polished presentation, the couple replaced their original policies and committed **$35,000 per year** in total premiums, set to continue for at least 15 years. The new policies had increasing death benefit structures, starting at **$400,000 for the husband and $450,000 for the wife, as their previous coverages for each.**

CHALLENGE: Just one year into the new policies, the couple began to have doubts. Their retirement investments had performed far better and did not have the high costs associated with the two policies. They started questioning the logic of putting so much money into whole life plans instead of funding their retirement accounts as before.

To complicate matters, the wife **unexpectedly lost her job**, and her income had been the primary source for funding the new policies. With rising financial pressure and job uncertainty, they began to wonder if they had made a mistake.

While networking at a business event, the wife met an independent **retirement-focused investment advisor**, who quickly referred them to **LIR** for an objective and detailed policy review.

At the same time, a friend referred them to **another life insurance advisor**—this one recommended replacing the policies with **Indexed Universal Life (IUL) policies**, each with long-term care riders. The IUL strategy was attractive on the surface: **nearly half the cost** of the whole life policies, with potential for long-term growth.

However, LIR's comprehensive analysis revealed that the IUL option also came with **significant uncertainties**. These policies relied on market-driven performance and **a heavy dependence on the insurance company to maintain high caps and participation rates**. What's more, the cost of insurance (COI) will continue to increase. Over time, these variables **could result in significantly** poor cash value performance, policy lapse risk, or unexpected premium increases. Such outcomes **did not align** with the couple's desire for simplicity, predictability, and **guaranteed long-term death benefit value, nor their need for LTC coverage.**

Likewise, their current whole life policies weren't free from risk either. If future dividends weren't sustained or increased, the policies could require additional premium payments just to maintain coverage. **What made it worse was that it was poorly designed with 100% base coverage.**

At this point, the couple's goals were crystal clear: no more assumptions or projected coverage outcomes. They wanted clear guarantees of coverage, as long as they made their fixed, scheduled premium payments.

SOLUTION: While the IUL appeared to be a lower-cost alternative, it still required the couple to **bet on future performance and the life insurance company's rates, caps, costs, etc., to be favorable.** Fortunately, the interest rate environment at the time provided several competitive options from highly rated life insurance companies offering **Guaranteed Universal Life (GUL)** and **Guaranteed Whole Life** solutions.

These products offered the same coverage objectives at lower cost than traditional whole life, with **guaranteed premium structures**, long-term care riders, and **no performance risk** placed on the policyholder.

After reviewing all options, the couple selected a **Guaranteed Universal Life policy** for each spouse that:

- Included a **clear, indemnity-based LTC rider** (not reimbursement-based)
- Was **nearly half the cost** of their current whole life policies
- Was **only about 5% more** than the IUL option, but with **zero uncertainty**

They no longer had to worry about fluctuating dividends or volatile market-based assumptions.

RESULT: With LIR's **proven, client-first process**, the couple received not just a second opinion but a better solution that reflected their real needs and financial goals.

Because every solution at LIR is **custom-designed**, the final structure included:

- A **20-pay GUL policy for the husband**, guaranteed to age 95
- A **20-pay GUL policy for the wife**, guaranteed to age 100

These policies **eliminated the need for cash value accumulation**, which only added cost and complexity in their case. Instead, they could access the **death benefit dollar-for-dollar for long-term care**, and if partially utilized or not used, the remaining death benefit would be paid to their heirs.

TAKEAWAY: Many advisors prioritize selling specific products rather than truly aligning coverage with clients' evolving needs and goals. This case highlights the importance of seeking an **independent, objective second opinion** focused on simplicity, guarantees, and real protection, especially for retirees concerned about long-term care and preserving retirement assets. Guaranteed Universal Life policies with LTC riders can offer peace of mind with predictable costs, avoiding cash value risks tied to market performance or uncertain dividends.

CASE STUDY 3: When Assuming Can Lead to a Mistake - The High-Performing Small Business Owner

CASE: A successful small-business owner in his early 40s was **advised to purchase a personal cash value life policy to protect his growing family, business, and estate**. With strong cash flow and little understanding of how life insurance worked, he was referred to a broker who came highly recommended.

The broker sold him a **$4 million Indexed Universal Life (IUL)** policy, promoting it as a powerful investment strategy that could:

- Build long-term, tax-advantaged cash value
- Offer future borrowing potential to reinvest in the business
- Grow wealth with flexibility
- Provide life insurance protection

The policy required him to pay premiums of **$10,000 per month**. Trusting the advice, he committed to the policy without getting a second opinion or truly understanding the pros and cons of the policy type and how it was designed for him.

CHALLENGE: Three years later, the client's business experienced a slowdown due to rising interest rates and slowing sales. At the same time, he hired a new CPA to review both business and personal finances—a critical step for small business owners whose financial lives are deeply connected.

During the review, the CPA questioned the $10,000/month going into a life insurance policy that seemed to **lack strategic priority, especially**

when the client was not even contributing much to his 401(k) plan (only about $10,000 a year) and facing pressure on business cash flow.

The CPA recommended the client seek a **second opinion from a fiduciary life insurance professional** and referred him to LIR for a full evaluation of the policy and its fit with his financial goals.

SOLUTION: LIR performed a **comprehensive life insurance needs analysis** and reviewed the IUL policy details. The findings were clear:

- The client had been **sold a complex, high-cost product** that benefited the agent more than it supported the client's priorities; evident from the fact that the policy can be designed with much lower costs and fees to the client with the use of blended Term coverage.
- The policy relied on **high non-guaranteed illustrated returns** and favorable insurance company renewal rates and caps, making it unpredictable as a "great investment" short term or long term for the client.
- While the client could afford the premium, it wasn't the best use of capital, especially with **business growth as the main priority and planning goal.**
- What the client really needed was **affordable, adequate protection**, not a complicated cash value policy built on many assumptions of cash value accumulation and tax-free income potential in the future.

We recommended canceling the IUL and replacing it with a **20 to 35-year level term life insurance policy** that included:

- **Critical, chronic, and terminal illness** coverage riders
- **A guaranteed conversion option** up to age 75
- The **same $4 million** in death benefit coverage
- A dramatically lower monthly premium: **just $825/month**

RESULT: The client **surrendered the IUL**, recovered the little available cash value (after surrender charges), and implemented the new term policy.

- He saved over $9,000/month, freeing up capital for his business operations, retirement savings, and personal liquidity.
- He now has clear, guaranteed coverage that fully protects his family and business, with built-in flexibility for the future beyond age 75.

Both the client and his CPA were extremely satisfied, noting that the new plan is better aligned with both his **short-term needs and long-term goals**.

TAKEAWAY: Assuming complex life insurance products are the best fit without fully understanding them can lead to costly mistakes, especially for small business owners juggling multiple financial priorities. This case shows the value of a fiduciary, needs-based review that cuts through hype and complexity to deliver simple, affordable, and guaranteed protection aligned with real goals. **Lower-cost term coverage with living benefits often provides greater flexibility and better cash flow for growing businesses and families.**

CASE STUDY 4: The Policy That Almost Didn't Pay Out – The Danger of Not Working with a Great Life Insurance Company

A 72-year-old woman, a frequent traveler, had purchased a **$250,000 whole life insurance policy** nearly 25 years prior. The original life insurance company was later acquired by another life insurance company.

She passed away while visiting Puerto Rico. Her family, assuming the policy would pay out without issue, **submitted a claim—only to have it denied**. They then submitted new paperwork that was asked of them, only to be denied again.

Frustrated and confused, one of the family's financial advisors referred the daughters (the beneficiaries) to LIR to review the policy and assist with the claims process.

CHALLENGE: The claim denial presented multiple complications:

- The **death occurred outside the continental U.S.**, adding complexity to documentation and communication.
- The **insurance company had changed ownership**, creating additional layers of verification.
- The **two beneficiaries were not on good terms**, which made coordination and communication difficult.
- There was **no clear understanding** of why the claim had been denied, nor who at the insurance company was responsible for the claim's case, as there were different representatives involved according to the records.

To make progress, the family needed a neutral, experienced team to gather the facts, manage communication, and keep everyone aligned on the same goal: getting the death claim approved and paid.

SOLUTION: The LIR team followed the structured **claims advocacy process**:

1. **Interviewed all involved parties**, including both daughters and anyone with knowledge of the original policy.
2. **Requested and reviewed** the full policy contract, the original application, all correspondence, and claims-related documents from the insurance company.
3. **Conducted multiple conference calls** with the carrier to:
    - Identify the exact reasons for claim denial
    - Understand what documents were missing or deemed incomplete
    - Clarify who was making the final decision within the claims department and make sure to communicate directly with them.

We coordinated communication among all parties, ensuring clarity and consistency, and helped the family compile and submit all required documentation, including a workaround for a missing certified document that was causing part of the delay.

RESULT: Thanks to LIR's persistence, structure, and understanding of how insurance carriers operate, the claim was successfully **approved and paid** without the need to escalate to a life insurance claims attorney.

The two critical success factors were:

1. **Clear, consistent communication** among family members and insurance company personnel
2. **Understanding and fulfilling the insurer's documentation requirements**, even when original certified copies were hard to obtain

TAKEAWAY:

Choosing **a reputable, responsive life insurance company matters as much as the policy itself**. When claims get complicated—especially with policy transfers, cross-border events, or family disputes—having an experienced advocate who understands the insurer's processes and can coordinate communication is crucial. Persistence, clarity, and thorough documentation can make the difference between a denied claim and a successful payout, avoiding costly legal battles.

CASE STUDY 5: The Retirement Illustration Illusion – The Problem with Maximum Allowed Assumptions

CASE: A couple in their mid-50s each purchased a **separate $500,000 Indexed Universal Life (IUL)** policy 14 years ago, intending to use the cash value as a **tax-free source of retirement income** once they turned 60.

As they began working with their estate planning attorney to finalize their estate plan, they reviewed the actual performance of both policies and were **deeply disappointed**. The cash values were **nowhere near what was originally projected in the illustration their financial advisor presented**. Concerned, they asked their attorney and CPA for a referral to a specialist who could:

- Evaluate the policies' performances
- Determine if the plans could be improved
- Clarify whether the tax-free withdrawal strategy was still viable

They had assumed their premium contributions would grow **in line with the stock market** or at least perform similarly to their retirement accounts, but reality told a different story.

CHALLENGE: After making premium payments on **two policies** for 14 years, the couple had counted on strong cash value growth to fund part of their retirement. Now, with retirement approaching, they feared they had **lost over a decade of time**—and possibly made the wrong financial decision.

Additional obstacles:

- Their **original agent** was no longer in the business and had left them with no one to turn to.
- They couldn't reach anyone at the insurance company who could **clearly explain the policy performance** or design flaws.
- They were unsure whether to **fix, replace, or cancel** the policies, and were concerned about the financial and tax implications of each option.

SOLUTION: The LIR team conducted a full analysis on **both IUL policies** by collecting:

- Each policy contract
- Original applications and product materials
- Initial sales illustrations and current in-force illustrations

We discovered:

- Both policies were **inefficiently designed**, to begin with:
    - High base death benefits and **no blended term riders**, resulting in **higher policy charges and expenses for the coverage amount**
    - Cap rates had **declined significantly** over time
    - Index selections had **underperformed** the backtested performances in the original illustrations
- The policies' actual internal rate of return (IRR) was **substantially lower** than what was assumed when the couple bought them
- Approximately **35% of their premiums were consumed by the costs**, severely limiting long-term accumulation

Instead of recommending replacements (which would reset their **10-year surrender schedules** and introduce new front-loaded policy costs), we explained the consequences, much like **refinancing a 30-year mortgage after 14 years**: it may reduce short-term payments, but it increases the total long-term cost and more years of payment to pay off the loan.

We advised **optimizing the current policies** instead:

- **Reduced both death benefits** to lower future cost-of-insurance charges
- **Reallocated the index selections** to improve potential performance
- Set up **annual reviews** to track and adjust as needed

We also introduced a complementary strategy: opening **Roth 401(k) accounts** for both spouses. This gave them additional **tax-free retirement funding** options, without the high costs embedded in their IUL policies.

By comparing their effective tax rate of approximately 23% to the internal policy charges, which consumed nearly 35% of their premium contributions, it became evident that the IUL policies they were sold were not a cost-effective solution for retirement income planning. The high fees and underperformance significantly undermined their original expectations, making alternative strategies like Roth 401(k)s a more efficient and transparent option moving forward.

RESULT:

- Both IUL policies were **salvaged and restructured** for better performance

- Unnecessary **death benefit was reduced to cut policy costs**
- **Reallocations to the S&P 500 index to better** align with market growth
- The couple **established and contributed to Roth 401(k)s** for lower-cost, and tax-free retirement growth
- Ongoing policy monitoring was implemented to **keep the plan on track**

When life insurance policies are sold based on overly optimistic assumptions and misunderstood tax strategies, clients are often left with **underperforming and misunderstood policies. Without ongoing reviews with a qualified advisor, these policies can silently drift off course until it's too late to fix them.**

TAKEAWAY: Life insurance illustrations often present optimistic assumptions that may not reflect real policy performance. **Overpromised projections can lead to costly misunderstandings and missed financial goals.** Regular, independent policy reviews are essential to catch design flaws, mange the costs, adjust the index allocation as needed. Combining insurance with other tax-efficient retirement plan options, like Roth 401(k)s, can create a more balanced and efficient financial plan, protecting their future without overpaying and relying heavily on a cash value life insurance policy.

CASE STUDY 6: The Free Look Period Saves a Family Estate From a Costly Mistake

CASE: A financial advisor's wealthy uncle recently purchased a $15 million whole life insurance policy with an annual premium of $930,000 for 7 years. **With only about 10 days left in the 30-day free look period**, the advisor became concerned that the policy was too expensive and may not even guarantee coverage through age 90. He sought an independent review to better understand the drawbacks and explore potential alternatives before the cancellation window closed.

CHALLENGE: Time was tight. There were fewer than 10 days remaining before the free look period expired. To complicate matters, the financial advisor had a delicate relationship with his uncle and wanted to ensure that any review would be handled with care. The uncle insisted that any meeting include both a representative from LIR and the insurance agent who sold him the policy—someone he trusted, who had over 35 years of experience and held the CLU® and ChFC® designations. **The only time everyone could meet was just three days before the free look deadline.**

SOLUTION: During the in-person meeting, we reviewed the existing policy in detail. While there were many differing opinions, the facts were clear:

- The policy's current illustration showed that the **coverage could lapse** under certain dividend performance scenarios.
- **Dividends were not guaranteed,** and future reductions could lower the death benefit.

- The policy had **all base insurance coverage** and no term coverage blending.
- The client had only been shown one company's product—**no competitive analysis or alternative designs were provided.**
- There were **no proposals aimed at improving the internal rate of return** on either the cash value or the death benefit.

Given the clear issues, the client, still within the free look window, exercised his right to cancel the policy the very next day.

RESULT: The client **avoided being locked into a costly long-term commitment** and instead selected an Indexed Universal Life (IUL) policy that provided greater flexibility, over 30% lower costs, and more control over the policy's cash value. He declined the guaranteed whole life and guaranteed UL options because he preferred flexibility over fixed guarantees and was comfortable with the risks of fluctuating cap rates in exchange for longer-term growth potential of the indexes.

In the end, **the key wasn't about choosing what the insurance agent or advisor thought was "best," but about ensuring the client had clear options and a thorough understanding of all the pros and cons of the policy design.** Empowered by that knowledge, he made a decision that perfectly aligned with his objective, walking away confident, satisfied, and in control of his financial planning.

TAKEAWAY: The free look period offers a powerful and often underutilized opportunity to reassess a life insurance purchase before making a long-term financial commitment. **An independent, thorough review during this time can reveal overlooked risks, excessive fees, and**

more suitable alternatives that better align with a client's overall financial strategy. By seeking objective advice and understanding all available options, consumers can make confident, informed decisions that support their long-term planning goals—before it's too late to pivot.

CASE STUDY 7: Got Sold a Life Policy and Got Recruited To Sell To Friends & Family

CASE: A young married couple in their early 30s was initially sold matching 20-year term life insurance policies. At the same time, the wife was persuaded by the insurance sales person to join his sales organization and start selling similar policies to her friends and family. It seemed like a **simple way to help others while earning some extra income on the side**.

However, while studying for her life insurance license, she was introduced to another insurance agent affiliated with a different life insurance marketing organization. This new group offered a wider range of life insurance products, including various types of cash value policies with living benefits. She was persuaded that this new organization presented a better opportunity, with more product options, higher compensation, and greater potential to help others.

Once she switched organizations, she replaced both her and her husband's term policies with Indexed Universal Life (IUL) policies that included living benefits. With the new training and sales support, she was able to **sell a few policies to her network, but she was not very active, as she had a full-time job.**

Four years later, shortly after the COVID pandemic, while having their taxes done with a new CPA they had been referred to, the couple asked for a referral to obtain a second opinion on their life insurance policies. They wanted to make sure their coverage was still appropriate, especially as they began planning to buy a home and wanted to access some of the cash value.

CHALLENGE: The couple had originally purchased the IUL policies as a way to accumulate tax-deferred cash value, intended to supplement their future retirement income. The living benefits feature would also allow them access to the death benefit in case of a chronic, critical, or terminal illness.

Despite the wife being licensed and having some training, **neither of them fully understood how their IUL policies were structured**—or if they were well-designed for their long-term retirement goals. They never received clear answers to their questions about its growth potential, and they mostly relied on what they were told and the illustrations that were presented to them.

They had never worked with an independent, fiduciary professional to objectively evaluate their policies or explore other options.

SOLUTION: To move forward with clarity, we had them complete a comprehensive life insurance needs analysis and submit copies of their policy contracts, original applications, and sales illustrations. Upon review, we discovered several issues:

- Their **choices were limited from the start** by the product focus of the marketing organization, which emphasized high-commission IUL policies with living benefits.
- The policy designs had such **high internal costs from policy charges and expenses** that the anticipated "tax-free" income from the policy loans would actually **cost more than twice the tax savings benefits compared to any other traditional investments.**

- Their cost of insurance was significantly higher than comparable products and was set to **increase steeply in their later retirement years**, a known issue with IUL policies.
- **The couple's actual insurance needs were straightforward**—providing affordable protection for each other's income replacement, mortgage coverage, and to have living benefits coverage in case of critical, chronic or terminal illness.

We recommended replacing the IULs with **35-year term life policies with conversion options** for each spouse that included **living benefits**. This provided them with the appropriate coverage at a **fraction of the cost**. The savings would allow them to **open and fund both Roth IRAs and Roth 401(k)s if they chose to, providing a much more cost-efficient and flexible path to a truly tax-free retirement, with plan costs of around 1%, compared to** the 35% average charges embedded in their original IULs.

RESULT: By seeking an **independent, fiduciary review**, the couple gained a crystal-clear understanding of their policies, the true costs involved, and the better options available to better fit in their financial planning priorities.

This case highlights **how easily well-meaning individuals can fall into commission-driven sales marketing businesses** that limit choices and place consumers at a disadvantage. Once removed from the pressure of peer influence, and sales incentives, they were able to focus on **transparency, cost-efficiency, and alignment with their actual financial goals**.

Ultimately, they made decisions based on what was truly right for their financial future, not on what someone else was incentivized to sell as "best" for them.

TAKEAWAY: Many families make life insurance decisions based on **trust, convenience, or existing relationships**, not necessarily based on **what's best for their long-term financial goals**. In this case, a well-meaning wife got involved in the insurance business, was trained to sell what her organization offered.

Despite being a licensed agent, she didn't fully understand how the policies worked or how the internal costs would impact future performance. **They trusted the company and the people, but never received a truly independent, expert review**.

The reality? Their IULs were expensive, inefficient, and misaligned with their core goals of mortgage protection and future income planning.

The good news: By seeking a second opinion, they discovered that a **low-cost, 35-year term policy with living benefits**—combined with the option to max out **Roth IRA and/or Roth 401(k)** accounts—would provide far better coverage and tax-free income potential, at a fraction of the cost.

Bottom line: Just because someone can sell life insurance doesn't mean they are qualified to design the right plan for your needs. **Policy design matters. Independent review matters. Your financial future deserves both.**

CASE STUDY 8: The Premium Financed Policy That Ends Up Costing More and Having Less Cash Value For Income

In 2018, a husband was sold one of the most widely marketed premium finance plans available to agents, brokers, and financial advisors. The plan was promoted as a "free bank-financed life insurance policy" and described as "low-to-no-risk"—**a pitch that made it sound too good to pass up**. He was told that by financing premiums for a particular Indexed Universal Life (IUL) policy plan, he could enjoy tax-free retirement income later, with little out-of-pocket cost, as the bank would provide the majority of the capital funding.

Following the premium-financed life insurance plan, after completing his final premium $50,000 payment in year five, the client grew curious about how the policy had actually performed versus the original illustrations. He asked his investment advisor, who handles his retirement investment accounts, for an opinion. That advisor referred the case to LIR for an independent and comprehensive policy analysis.

CHALLENGE: The client had completed the full premium funding schedule of five years as planned, so at this point, there was very little room to modify or restructure the policy. However, he did maintain excellent documentation, including the original sales illustration and communications from the agent. This allowed LIR to do a side-by-side comparison between the **original projections** and the **current in-force illustration**.

Unfortunately, the findings were disappointing:

- Despite strong stock market performance over the past five years since 2018 (the S&P 500 gained over 80% during that time), the policy's actual values fell **below even the original worst-case scenario** projection during the time of the "Great Depression".
- Cap rates on the IUL had declined significantly since the policy was issued, and **interest rates on the loan increased higher than originally illustrated**.
- The current return trajectory showed **no meaningful improvement** going forward—even in a high interest rate environment, the cap rates continued trending lower, creating a drag on policy growth.

SOLUTION: Since the premium finance arrangement was already in place and the funding was complete, the client was locked in. The best course of action was to **monitor the policy annually**, request updated in-force illustrations, and look for any potential changes or improvements based on market or crediting rate shifts.

What this case highlights is the **need for extreme caution** when dealing with complex life insurance strategies, especially those sold as "simple" or "guaranteed" to generate tax-free retirement income. Sales presentations often downplay the complexities and the risks, and in this case, the client was not shown alternative retirement income planning options other than a very specific IUL product.

In reality, after accounting for borrowing costs, lower cap rates, and delayed income, the client's expected return fell to around **1.5% annually**, far below expectations. A simple Time Value of Money (TVM) or Internal Rate of Return (IRR) analysis shows the client may have been better off placing his contributions in a high yielding money market or balanced brokerage account, with **less complexity and more liquidity**.

RESULT: There is no easy way to unwind the current policy. The client's funds are now **tied up for at least another 15 years**, and when the time comes to begin withdrawing tax-free income, the current projected amount is now about **40% less** than originally projected.

The only meaningful benefit remaining is the death benefit, which, ironically, was never the client's primary goal. He was sold on the promise of high tax-free income in his retirement years. Unfortunately, the outcome highlights the importance of seeking **independent, fiduciary-level advice** before entering into complex insurance strategies, particularly when tax-advantaged long-term retirement income is the primary objective.

TAKEAWAY: Premium finance strategies are often marketed as a smart way to get "free life insurance" or "tax-free retirement income." But as this case shows, **complex doesn't mean better, and "simple" sales pitches often hide real risks**.

Despite strong stock market performance, this client's premium financed IUL underperformed even its worst-case projections. Rising loan interest rates, falling cap rates, and high internal costs all eroded the policy's value, leaving the client locked into a long-term, low-return commitment with little flexibility.

The true cost? Lost time, lost opportunity, and a projected long term **internal rate of return (IRR) below 2%**—far less than what could've been achieved with even a conservative investment strategy.

The lesson: **If you don't fully understand how a strategy works—especially one involving loans and life insurance—it's critical to get an independent review from a fiduciary-level expert before moving forward.** Once you're locked in, the options for course correction are often very limited.

Even sophisticated investors can be misled by polished presentations. That's why an independent second opinion can be one of the most valuable financial decisions you make.

CASE STUDY 9: Buying a Life Insurance Policy from the Same Insurance Company That Paid Out on Dad's Policy

CASE: A 53-year-old husband and his 51-year-old wife recently purchased a **$5,000,000 survivorship whole life policy** using the life insurance proceeds the husband received after his father passed away. His father had left him approximately the same amount, and now, wanting to carry forward that legacy, the husband hoped to leave $2.5 million to each of his two sons through his own estate plan.

They went to the same life insurance company that paid out on his father's policy to buy a similar policy, and the assigned agent simply asked for their **annual premium budget**, which they said was approximately **$70,000–$75,000**, based on their municipal bond investment income. Unsurprisingly, the whole life policy they were sold had an annual premium of **$72,000**, exactly within their stated budget, but with **no side-by-side comparison** of other products or strategies.

The couple was later referred to LIR by a friend who worked at a captive insurance agency specializing in home and auto coverage. While this friend didn't have expertise in complex life insurance planning, they strongly encouraged the couple to seek an **independent, fiduciary-level second opinion**—just to be sure.

CHALLENGE: The clients had already placed the policy inside an **Irrevocable Life Insurance Trust (ILIT)**, drafted by an estate planning attorney referred by the original agent. They were making their scheduled premium payments and sending **Crummey Letters** each year as instructed—but they admitted they didn't fully understand the policy's details, how it was structured, or whether it was truly the best option for their estate plan.

They had several key concerns:

- Would reviewing or replacing the policy interfere with the ILIT?
- Could the estate plan be disrupted by making a change?
- Was it even possible to get a better policy now that it had already been in place for nearly a year?

Most importantly, they feared no one outside the original sales team could give them truly **independent guidance** that accounted for both the policy *and* the trust structure.

SOLUTION: The LIR team took a **collaborative approach**, working directly with the clients and their estate planning attorney to:

- **Confirm there were no restrictions** in the ILIT preventing policy replacement.
- **Obtain in-force illustrations** from the current carrier to analyze performance after nearly one year.
- **Verify the clients' health status** to ensure eligibility for new coverage.
- **Shop the entire market**, quoting all available survivorship options, including both **Whole Life** and **Indexed Universal Life (IUL)**, across **guaranteed and non-guaranteed** designs.
- Conduct an **Internal Rate of Return (IRR) analysis** to compare the true cost-efficiency of various solutions.

RESULT: Thanks to LIR's extensive expertise, which includes not only seasoned insurance professionals but also **an in-house estate planning attorney and two CPAs**, we were able to offer a far superior solution.

Instead of one policy, we recommended **two separate survivorship policies** using two A+ rated mutual life insurance companies. Because the wife qualified for **more favorable underwriting**, splitting the coverage helped lower costs. The outcome:

- Total death benefit increased to **$7 million ($2 million more)**, guaranteed to at least age 95 (on the younger spouse).
- **Annual premium reduced to approximately $49,000**—a savings of more than $23,000 per year.
- The **premiums are for only 20 years**, as opposed to continuous premiums being required in the previous policy.
- Coverage is diversified between **two top-rated carriers**, enhancing stability and flexibility.
- **No changes needed to the existing ILIT structure**—just proper documentation and coordination.

TAKEAWAY:

Because the clients had the foresight to verify their decision with an **independent, fiduciary resource**, they avoided locking into an unnecessarily expensive policy for decades to come. They gained significantly more **guaranteed death benefit**, **reduced premium costs**, and peace of mind knowing their estate plan was aligned with their financial goals.

This case is a powerful reminder that even policies sold with good intentions—or from companies with a personal relationship history from a parent—should still be **reviewed independently**. Trusting your gut and getting a second opinion can make a **seven-figure difference** in more value.

CASE STUDY 10: Converting a Whole Life Policy into a Long-Term Care Tax-Free Solution

CASE:

A 68-year-old client had purchased a whole life policy back in 1992. Over the decades, the policy had accumulated approximately **$65,000 in cash value** and maintained a total death benefit of about **$180,000**, much of which was made up of a **$175,000 term rider** blended into the $5,000 base policy. The client was in excellent health and expected to live well into his 90s. However, he no longer needed the death benefit and did **not want to pay any further premiums**.

His main concern was twofold:

1. **How long would the policy remain in force** without additional payments?
2. **Could he access the cash value later in life**, particularly if he needed it for **long-term care**, without jeopardizing the policy?

CHALLENGE: After multiple unsuccessful attempts to get answers from the insurance company and with no local agent available to assist, the client turned to Google and found LIR. He willingly paid for a **professional, fiduciary-level review** to get clarity on his options.

Given the age and unique structure of the policy, there was significant uncertainty around how future **costs of insurance**, especially those associated with the large term rider, would affect policy longevity. He was open to solutions but made it clear that his **priority was long-term care planning**, not a death benefit for his spouse or children.

SOLUTION: The team held several Zoom consultations with the client and conducted a detailed policy review, including a conference call with the insurance carrier to request customized **inforce illustrations** showing different premium payment scenarios and dividend assumptions. We also had the client complete a **comprehensive life insurance needs analysis**, which reaffirmed that **long-term care protection** was the most important priority moving forward.

Because we operate independently and are not beholden to any one company or product, we were able to present **a full range of long-term care annuity options**. The best fit was a **tax-free 1035 exchange** into a **guaranteed LTC-focused annuity**, which would **triple the value of his current cash value** for use toward long-term care expenses. If he doesn't use the LTC benefits, the remaining value would still be passed on to his beneficiaries.

RESULT: Thanks to LIR's **thorough, fiduciary process**, the client transitioned from an outdated policy that no longer aligned with his goals to a solution that gave him **confidence and guaranteed protection** for his future. His former insurance carrier could only offer basic projections and did not have a viable long-term care strategy. Our process empowered him to:

- **Stop paying premiums** on a policy he no longer needed
- **Preserve his $65,000 in cash value** through a 1035 exchange
- **Secure up to $195,000** in long-term care benefits
- **Retain control** over the cash value, which will go to his heirs if unused for long term care

This case proves how an **independent review can uncover powerful alternatives** that traditional carriers and captive agents simply don't offer.

TAKEAWAY: Too often, clients are left with outdated life insurance policies that no longer serve their current needs, and worse, they can't get clear answers from the original insurer or agents. This case highlights how a **thorough, independent review** can uncover powerful strategies like using a **1035 exchange** to convert an underutilized whole life policy into a **guaranteed, tax-free long-term care solution**, tripling its value for care needs while preserving any unused benefits for heirs. For clients nearing retirement, understanding **how to repurpose life insurance assets** can make all the difference in long-term security and peace of mind.

CASE STUDY 11: Don't Need Life Insurance Anymore? It Might Be Worth a Lot More Than You Think.

CASE: A 72-year-old client owned a **$600,000 term life insurance policy** with 5 months remaining on the conversion option. With both diabetes and a history of prostate cancer, the client no longer needed life insurance and had no interest in converting the policy. His original life insurance agent told him that if he wanted to sell it, the most he could expect was **$10,000 through a life settlement**.

CHALLENGE: The client was initially satisfied with the $10,000 offer and had very little motivation to explore other options. In fact, he was originally planning to let the policy lapse altogether. The biggest hurdle was helping the client see the **potential hidden value** of the policy, even though the process could take time. With some encouragement from his investment advisor and education from the LIR team, he agreed to conduct a full review and explore a life settlement more thoroughly.

SOLUTION: LIR took a **measured, step-by-step approach**, working not only with the client but also engaging his spouse and adult son to help guide him through the process. LIR explained that the $10,000 offer **he received was just a single bid**, not a reflection of true market value. LIR worked across multiple settlement providers, starting with three life settlement companies and later expanding to bring in additional competitive bids. The team coordinated medical underwriting updates, gathered all necessary documentation, and kept the client's family informed every step of the way.

RESULT: After approximately **3 months**, the client accepted a **final settlement offer of $50,000—five times more** than he initially expected. The process required patience and diligence, especially with the client's initial doubts, but in the end, he was thrilled with the outcome. What he once viewed as a "worthless" policy turned out to be a valuable asset that significantly strengthened his retirement savings.

TAKEAWAY: Most policyholders have no idea their term life insurance can be sold, even near the end of the conversion window, and that **multiple bids** from reputable life settlement providers can lead to **significantly higher payouts**. Relying solely on the original agent's input or a single offer can leave real money on the table. Independent, fiduciary-level review can **uncover hidden value in policies previously thought to be disposable**—and make the difference between walking away with nothing or with tens of thousands of dollars.

CASE STUDY 12: Non-Qualified Annuity to Fund a Survivorship Life Policy for Estate Planning

CASE: A 62-year-old client was referred to LIR by his Certified Financial Planner (CFP®). He owned a **non-qualified variable annuity valued at $403,000**, which had just exited a six-year surrender schedule. While the annuity had grown significantly—with **approximately $203,000 in gains**—the client **did not plan to use it for retirement income**.

Instead, he wanted to **leave the annuity's value to his children** or find a better way to support his **estate planning goals**. However, terminating the annuity would trigger a substantial tax liability, as the gains would be taxed as ordinary income.

CHALLENGE: The client was **highly tax-sensitive** and already had significant passive income and other financial assets. He didn't need income from the annuity now or in the future. Instead, he was focused on **transferring wealth efficiently** to the next generation and **covering an estimated $4 million estate tax liability**.

He had two primary options to consider:

1. **Complete a 1035 exchange into another annuity** to continue deferring taxes and avoid immediately recognizing the $203,000 in gains.
2. **Strategically repurpose the annuity** to fund as much of his estate plan as possible—in a way that maximized tax efficiency and wealth transfer.

SOLUTION: Because the LIR team includes professionals with expertise in **life insurance, estate planning, and tax strategies**, we collaborated with the client and his CFP® to design a customized solution that met multiple objectives.

We proposed the following plan:

- **1035 Exchange** the existing annuity into a new **variable annuity** with a specialized **"lifetime withdrawal rider."** This allowed the client to continue investing the funds while accessing approximately 5% per year in withdrawals, without triggering immediate taxation by LIFO (Last-In, First-Out) rule.
- Set up a **structured withdrawal plan of $20,000 per year** from the annuity to **fund a 20-pay Survivorship Guaranteed Universal Life (SGUL) policy**.
- The SGUL policy would:
  - Cost approximately **$400,000 total** over 20 years.
  - Provide a **guaranteed $2 million death benefit** (to age 100 for him and to age 110 for his spouse).
  - Be used explicitly to help **offset future estate tax liabilities**.
- The team conducted a thorough review of available products and selected the policy with the **highest internal rate of return (IRR)** for the given premium structure and death benefit—ensuring the most efficient use of the client's annuity funds.

RESULT: The client was able to **leverage his $403,000 non-qualified annuity** into a **guaranteed $2 million estate planning asset** without immediately incurring the large tax hit he was trying to avoid.

This solution provided:

- Tax deferral into another variable annuity with great flexibility
- New Annuity allows for annuitization tax-advantage like withdrawals but with better flexibility
- A clear and measurable return on investment for this new plan
- Satisfaction for both the client and his financial planner, who appreciated the strategic, tax-smart approach and the simplicity of the outcome.

TAKEAWAY: Estate planning requires more than just good intentions —it demands **proactive strategies, advanced product knowledge, and integrated financial planning.** By working with **fiduciary insurance professionals** who understand taxes, annuities, estate planning, and advanced life insurance design, clients can turn idle assets into powerful legacy tools. The key is seeking advice from a professional that delivers **independent analysis, product-neutral recommendations**, and customized strategies aligned with your long-term goals.

BONUS AND NOTES

10 QUESTIONS TO ASK *YOURSELF*

About Your Agent, Broker, or Financial Advisor

To protect yourself from being sold life insurance that may not be in your best interest.

- Do they seem more focused on selling me a life insurance product than helping me understand all of my financial options?
- Are they part of a company or marketing group that rewards sales volume, recruiting, or advancement through incentives? Could that be influencing their advice to me?
- Do they only have a life insurance license — but still call themselves a financial advisor or imply they're qualified to advise me on investments, taxes, and retirement planning?
- Do they claim to be a "broker," yet offer choices from only a few companies and product types, or operate through a company that markets life insurance products?
- Do they have experience in properly designing life insurance policies, strategies, and working with underwriting — or is their knowledge and experience more general/limited?
- Are they promoting a Cash-Value Life Insurance policy as a way to "grow money tax-free" or "create tax-free retirement income" — without clearly explaining the complexities, costs, trade-offs, and risks?
- Are they suggesting I reduce or stop contributions to my retirement accounts (401k/457/403b/IRA), or brokerage account in order to pay more premiums to a cash value life insurance or annuity product?
- Have they been fully transparent about how they're compensated, whether they earn commissions, and if they have sales incentives tied to specific products or companies?
- Did they provide the minimum required illustration pages— or just select pages that leave out important details? Ex. pages that disclose the annual policy charges & expenses and the internal rate of return (IRR) report.
- Did they clearly explain the Free Look Period (usually 10–30 days) and encourage me to review the final delivered policy in detail — or did they gloss over this important step when delivering the final policy?

If any of these questions gives you a feeling of uncertainty, it may be time to pause — and seek a second opinion from an independent, fiduciary-level professional.

Red, Yellow, & Green "Life Insurance" Decision Guide™

Cash Value Life Insurance — Designed for CASH VALUE ACCUMULATION

Strong Reasons NOT to Buy for Cash Value Growth

(STOP: very poor fit for accumulation goals)

- **You haven't maxed tax-advantaged investments (Roth 401(k), Roth IRA, HSA, SEP, Solo 401(k), etc.).** These typically offer better growth, lower costs, and simpler rules.
- **Short time horizon (<10 yrs).** High charges and expenses in early policy years can delay break-even to around year 5 or 6.
- **You'll need liquidity soon.** Surrender charges + slow early cash value buildup make this a poor near-term savings vehicle.
- **High-interest debt outstanding.** Paying 18% on cards while funding a policy targeting mid-single-digit long-term IRR is backwards.
- **You can't commit to consistent premium funding / overfunding.** Underfunded policies underperform and may lapse.
- **You don't understand (or won't monitor) policy loans.** Mismanaged loans can implode policies and create unexpected tax bills.

Possible Fit, But Requires Careful Design & Ongoing Management

(YIELD: proceed with analysis, testing, and realistic expectations)

- **Supplemental tax-advantaged bucket after other accounts are funded.** Works only if premiums are sized to avoid MEC (unless MEC status is acceptable).
- **Desire for conservative, bond-alternative accumulation with downside buffers.** Indexed UL or whole life may appeal—but internal costs matter.
- **You value long-term tax-deferred growth + potential tax-free access via loans.** Must track basis, maintain funding, and manage loan rates vs. crediting.
- **You want diversification away from market volatility.** Understand crediting methods, caps, participation rates, dividends—not guaranteed.
- **You're comfortable funding at/near guideline premium limits to improve efficiency.** Policy must be properly structured (low base, high PUA/overfunded design depending on chassis).
- **You're comparing policies already in-force vs. new design.** 1035 exchange analysis, surrender charges, loan transfers, and tax implications must be reviewed.

Strong Case to Use a Policy Optimized for Accumulation

(GO: clear to explore and design)

- **All core financial foundations covered:** Emergency fund, debt managed, retirement plans maximized.
- **Stable, high, predictable cash flow to overfund policy early.** Front-loading improves long-term internal rate of return.
- **Long time horizon (10+ yrs) and intent to keep policy in force.** Compounding, dividends/credited interest, and cost smoothing require time.
- **You plan disciplined policy management:** Annual review of charges, crediting, policy performance, loan strategy.
- **You want tax-advantaged supplemental retirement income in later years** (policy loan/withdraw-to-basis design modeled conservatively).
- **You benefit from state-level creditor protection of cash values** (varies by jurisdiction; confirm).

Quick Comparsion Chart

Goal	Best Design Tends To Be	Key Design Focus	Main Funding Style	Primary Risk If Mismanaged
Cash Value Accumulation	**Overfunded WL, IUL, VUL (low cost design)**	**Maximize premium efficiency / minimize drag**	**Front-load to guideline limits**	**Underperformance / policy lapse / poor IRR**
Permanent/Max Death Benefit	WL, GUL, No-lapse IUL, VUL, Survivorship type	Lifetime NLG (no-lapse guarantee) or estate liquidity	Level premiums; may use premium financing	Lapse risk if guarantee terms not met; estate shortfall

Red, Yellow, & Green "Life Insurance" Decision Guide™

Cash Value Life Insurance — Designed for PERMANENT/MAX DEATH BENEFIT

Strong Reasons NOT to Buy for Lifetime Death Benefit

(STOP: Permanent coverage is not warranted)

- **Your need is temporary (income replacement while kids are young, mortgage payoff window).** Term insurance is far more cost-effective.
- **Budget is tight.** Permanent policies require higher, long-term premiums. Underfunded policies often lapse or demand more premiums, effectively wasting the premiums already paid.
- **You have no legacy, estate, business continuity, or liquidity goals beyond your working years.** No permanent need = no permanent policy required.
- **You are older and cost-per-$ death benefit is prohibitive vs. alternatives** (Guaranteed UL or no-lapse IUL or VUL may be cost-effective.
- **You're treating it as an "investment" without understanding costs and returns.** Permanent policies are poor investment vehicles due to high fees, slow to no growth, and uncertain returns.
- **You're being sold on "you'll lose coverage when term expires" fear tactics** without modeling laddered term or conversion strategies.

Death Benefit May Be Needed, But Design Carefully

(YIELD: clarify purpose, funding, guarantees)

- **Estate liquidity concerns but uncertain future estate size.** Run projections for federal & state estate tax thresholds; consider ILIT ownership.
- **Illiquid assets (real estate, business, farm) that heirs may need to equalize.** Need sizing, ownership structure, and premium funding plan.
- **Special-needs dependent or long-term care obligation.** Must coordinate with trusts, government benefit eligibility, and rider features.
- **You're transitioning from large term policies nearing conversion deadlines.** Compare converting vs. new permanent vs. blend.
- **Desire for lifetime guarantee but also some cash value access.** Balance between Guaranteed UL (cheaper, less cash) and WL / IUL / VUL (flexible, less guarantee certainty).
- **Multi-insured strategies (second-to-die / survivorship).** Useful for estate equalization but must model timing of estate tax liability.

Clear Permanent/Maximum Death Benefit Use Cases

(GO: clear to explore and design)

- **Estate liquidity funding** to cover estate taxes, equalize inheritances, or keep family businesses intact while maximizing the death benefit for heirs.
- **Special-needs child or dependent protection** where guaranteed funds must exist, ensuring the maximum death benefit regardless of when you pass away.
- **Irrevocable Life Insurance Trust (ILIT) strategies** to remove proceeds from the taxable estate and ensure the highest benefit value is transferred efficiently.
- **Business succession or buy-sell planning** where a guaranteed payout (1st-to-die or 2nd-to-die) with maximum coverage secures ownership continuity.
- **Charitable legacy planning,** leveraging the premium-to-death benefit multiple to amplify charitable gifts while replacing donated wealth to heirs.
- **You've outlived term coverage, still need protection, and are healthy enough** to lock in lifetime coverage and maximizing death benefit value before health declines.

Quick Comparsion Chart

Goal	Best Design Tends To Be	Key Design Focus	Main Funding Style	Primary Risk If Mismanaged
Cash Value Accumulation	Overfunded WL, IUL, VUL (low cost design)	Maximize premium efficiency / minimize drag	Front-load to guideline limits	Underperformance / policy lapse / poor IRR
Permanent/Max Death Benefit	**WL, GUL, No-lapse IUL, VUL, Survivorship type**	**Lifetime NLG (no-lapse guarantee) or estate liquidity**	**Level premiums; may use premium financing**	**Lapse risk if guarantee terms not met; estate shortfall**

Red, Yellow, & Green "Life Insurance" Decision Guide™

TERM Life with LIVING BENEFITS & CONVERSION OPTION

When This Design Is NOT a Good Fit

Your top priority is the lowest premium.
- Living benefits and conversion features increase cost compared to basic term.

You're certain your coverage need is short-term.
- Paying for extra flexibility doesn't make sense if coverage will end in 5–10 years.

You already own permanent coverage.
- A conversion feature adds no value if lifetime protection is already secured.

You don't plan to use the living benefits or conversion feature.
- Paying extra for features you'll never use is wasted cost.

Proceed with Caution

You assume living benefits cover all health events.
- Only specific critical, chronic, or terminal illnesses qualify.

You plan to convert but can't realistically afford permanent premiums later.
- Conversion is only valuable if you can maintain it.

You may not understand the conversion window.
- Many policies have deadlines for converting without underwriting.

You are comparing only premium cost, not value.
- The extra benefits may be worth it, but only if aligned with your goals.

Best Fit Scenarios

You want future-proof coverage flexibility.
- Convertibility protects your insurability, regardless of future health.

You value living benefits for critical, chronic, or terminal illness.
- Accessing a portion of the death benefit can be a financial lifesaver.

You're young and healthy but want long-term options later.
- Low-cost term now, with the ability to upgrade later, is strategic.

You anticipate major life changes.
- Ideal if marriage, kids, or business planning could create a permanent coverage need.

Bottom Line Comparison – Term Life Insurance Designs

Design	Premium Cost	Living Benefits	Convertibility	Flexibility for Future Needs	Death Benefit per Premium $	Best For
Term with Living Benefits & Conversion	**Slightly higher due to added features**	**Yes – Chronic, Critical, Terminal illness access**	**Yes – Upgrade to permanent without a new medical exam**	**High – Future-proof coverage**	**Slightly less due to rider costs**	**Those wanting flexibility, future planning, and health protection**
Basic Term (No Conversion)	Lowest possible cost	No – Death benefit only	No – Must re-qualify for new coverage	None – Coverage ends at term	Maximum per premium dollar	Those needing pure, temporary coverage at the lowest cost

Red, Yellow, & Green "Life Insurance" Decision Guide™

TERM Life with NO CONVERSION OPTION/BASIC

When This Design Is NOT a Good Fit

You might want permanent coverage later.
- No conversion option means you could be uninsurable when term ends.

You want added living benefit features.
- Basic term is death benefit only, with no health-based payout options.

You're focusing on cost alone.
- Cheaper premiums may cost more long-term if coverage needs change.

Proceed with Caution

You assume you can always buy new coverage later.
- Age and health changes may make that impossible or very expensive.

You're using term for a long-term need.
- Without conversion, you could lose coverage when you need it most.

You're comparing price without factoring value.
- Flexibility and living benefits may be worth slightly higher premiums.

Best Fit Scenarios

You have a short-term, defined need.
- Perfect for covering a mortgage, loans, or temporary financial obligations.

You're confident in your health and future insurability.
- Basic term is fine if you expect to renew or replace coverage later.

You need the maximum death benefit for the lowest cost.
- Ideal when budget is tight and flexibility is less important.

Bottom Line Comparison – Term Life Insurance Designs

Design	Premium Cost	Living Benefits	Convertibility	Flexibility for Future Needs	Death Benefit per Premium $	Best For
Term with Living Benefits & Conversion	Slightly higher due to added features	Yes – Chronic, Critical, Terminal illness access	Yes – Upgrade to permanent without a new medical exam	High – Future-proof coverage	Slightly less due to rider costs	Those wanting flexibility, future planning, and health protection
Basic Term (No Conversion)	**Lowest possible cost**	**No – Death benefit only**	**No – Must re-qualify for new coverage**	**None – Coverage ends at term**	**Maximum per premium dollar**	**Those needing pure, temporary coverage at the lowest cost**

LIFE INSURANCE™
REVIEW.com

Dear Policyholder,

I am your life insurance policy. Though I remain quietly in the background, my purpose is deeply aligned with yours—to provide for your needs and for the ones you love, especially when you no longer can.

Today, it is your responsibility to provide for your family and loved ones. As you fulfill that important role, I stand ready—made possible by your foresight and commitment—and prepared for the day when I must step forward and carry that responsibility in your place.

Because of your careful diligence—your research, thoughtful questions, and thorough verification—you can be confident that I am the right policy for your needs. You did not rush. You did not guess. You made an informed, intentional decision. And because of that, you can move forward with peace of mind, knowing your family is protected by a plan that truly fits.

There may be moments when the cost of maintaining me feels like just another obligation. But remember: I am not just a policy—I am a promise. One day, when your journey ends, mine will begin—supporting your loved ones with the care, stability, and protection you planned for all along. And if life brings unexpected hardship while you are still here, I may even be able to step in early—because that, too, is part of the promise.

You've done your part with care and intention, so there is no need for doubt. You chose wisely—and I will be here, ready when the time comes.

With enduring purpose,

Your Life Insurance Policy

www.LifeInsuranceReview.com

NOTES

- Download the Don't be sold-Empowerment Kit by using this link: lifeinsurancereview.com/free-look-period
- Use the exclusive code LIRBOOKFINISH to receive 25% off all LIR services.
-

www.ingramcontent.com/pod-product-compliance
Lightning Source LLC
LaVergne TN
LVHW050928210926
848482LV00013B/573
* 9 7 9 8 2 1 8 7 5 1 8 3 8 *